A Practical Guide to Claims Arising From Accidents Abroad and Travel Claims

Andrew Mckie,
Barrister at Law, Clerksroom (Manchester),
LLB Hons, PG DIP and
Former Solicitor Advocate,
Personal Injury, Fraud, Credit Hire

and

Ian Skeate, Barrister at Law, Clerksroom
(Manchester),
BA/MA (Cantab), Personal Injury, Costs,
Disciplinary/Regulatory Work

Law Brief Publishing

Published 2017 by
Law Brief Publishing
30 The Parks
Minehead
Somerset
TA24 8BT

www.lawbriefpublishing.com

Paperback: 978-1-911035-02-2

PREFACE

The Jackson reforms of 2013 have placed significant pressure on personal injury law firms. With the proposed changes to the small claims track, law firms are having to look other areas of personal injury law. One such area of law is accidents abroad and travel claims. This text follows on from the first text 'A Practical Guide to Holiday Sickness Claims'.

The writers are both self-employed Personal Injury Barristers and joint owners of a BSB Regulated entity, that undertakes accidents abroad and travel claims. Looking at the literature available in this area, it struck us that there are very few practical texts dealing with accidents abroad and travel litigation that are designed in a practical and easy to navigate manner.

This book therefore looks at all aspects of the claims process for accidents abroad and travel claims from cradle to grave. The book covers all aspects of accidents abroad including but not limited to claims under the 1992 Package Travel Regulations, accidents on ships, accidents on planes, accidents on tour operator excursions, ski/snowboard accidents, quantum and causation in travel claims, and costs.

The aim of this book is to provide a concise but comprehensive guide to this area of practice, that can be utilised by practitioners on a day-to-day basis, in Claimant and Defendant practices.

The book has a focus on running accidents abroad and travel claims in an efficient way post-Jackson, spotting the winners and vetting the losing claims early on.

We would encourage the reader to 'dip in and out' of the book as and when required.

We wish to thank Tim Kevan of Law Brief publishing for providing me with the opportunity to write this book and for the PI Brief update website for publishing relevant sections.

Andrew Mckie
Personal Injury Barrister
Clerksroom

Ian Skeate
Personal Injury Barrister
Clerksroom

February 2017

Contents

CHAPTER ONE
CLAIMS UNDER THE PACKAGE TRAVEL REGULATIONS 1992

The Package Travel, Package Holidays and Package Tours Regulations 1992 – What is a Package? – Telephone Bookings

One of the key matters that will always need to be looked at in accident abroad claims, is whether the 1992 Regulations apply or not. This Chapter deals with bookings made by telephone and in a face to face meeting at the office of the tour operator / travel agents. Internet bookings will be dealt with below.

Claims brought under the 1992 Regulations, allow a consumer to sue in contract in England and Wales for an accident case which may have incurred outside the jurisdiction. This is extremely useful and convenient as it avoids the procedural difficulties of litigating outside the jurisdiction of England and Wales as well as imposing on the Defendant UK standards. In these cases the practitioner will be relieved to know that the procedural and evidential rules used will be that of English law and the Civil Procedure Rules.

The Regulations impose duties upon Tour Operators.

Regulation 3 says:-

> "*Application of Regulations*
>
> *3. (1) These Regulations apply to packages sold or offered for sale in the territory of the United Kingdom.*
>
> *(2) Regulations 4 to 15 apply to packages so sold or offered for sale on or after 31st December 1992.*
>
> *(3) Regulations 16 to 22 apply to contracts which, in whole or part, remain to be performed on 31st December 1992".*

An example of a service that is 'ancillary' for the purposes of the Regulations would be the provision of food and drink on board an aircraft.

The full Regulations can be found at:-
http://www.legislation.gov.uk/uksi/1992/3288/made

What is a Package?

> "*The definition of a package within the meaning of the Regulations is as follows:-*
>
> "*The pre-arranged combination of at least two of the following components when sold or offered for sale at an inclusive price and when the service covers a period of more than twenty-four hours or includes overnight accommodation:—*
>
> *a) transport;*
> *b) accommodation*
> *c) other tourist services not ancillary to transport or accommodation and accounting for a significant proportion of the package,*
>
> *and*
>
> *(i) the submission of separate accounts for different components shall not cause the arrangements to be other than a package;*
>
> *(ii) the fact that a combination is arranged at the request of the consumer and in accordance with his specific instructions (whether modified or not) shall not of itself cause it to be treated as other than pre-arranged;*
>
> *and*
>
> "*retailer" means the person who sells or offers for sale the package put together by the organizer".*

In *R (on the application of ASSOCIATION OF BRITISH TRAVEL AGENTS LTD (ABTA)) (CLAIMANT) v CIVIL AVIATION AUTHORITY (DEFENDANT) & SECRETARY OF STATE FOR TRADE & INDUSTRY (INTERESTED PARTY)(CLAIMANT) v CIVIL AVIATION AUTHORITY (DEFENDANT) & SECRETARY OF STATE FOR TRADE & INDUSTRY (INTERESTED PARTY) (2006) [2006] EWCA Civ 1356*, the Court looked at the question as to the meaning of a package within the Regulations. It said:-

> *22. "At first sight, therefore, there is now little, if anything, bsetween the parties on this question. The requirement that the components be sold or offered for sale "at an inclusive price" must be read in conjunction with the requirement that the components be sold or offered for sale as a pre-arranged combination. The price is the price of the combination.*
>
> *25. In many cases – indeed, I suspect, in the majority of cases – the price of the combination will not be the aggregate of the prices for which the components within the combination would have been sold or offered for sale if each component had been sold or offered for sale as a separate service outside the combination. That may be because some of the components (for example, the services of the organiser's local representative) would not be available as a separate service outside the combination. Or it may be because some of the components can be provided more cheaply if provided in conjunction with other components - the hotel may provide a courtesy airport transfer service. Or it may be that, in order to sell the package, the organiser will price attractively: the organiser will offer the package of services at a price which is below the aggregate of the prices which would be charged if the components had been sold separately. In those cases there is unlikely to be difficulty in reaching the conclusion, on the facts, that the components (including flight accommodation) are being sold as a pre-arranged combination and at an inclusive price. The same could be said of cases – which, I suspect, are likely to be rare indeed – in which the price of the com-*

bination exceeds the aggregate of the prices for which the components would have been sold or offered for sale separately.

26. The more difficult cases are those in which the price for the whole is equal to the aggregate of the prices for which the components would have been sold or offered for sale separately. The principle is, perhaps, easier to state than to apply in practice. If the components are offered for sale as a pre-arranged combination – albeit that the components are not combined (and, perhaps, not all identified) until "the moment when the parties reach an agreement and conclude the contract" (to adopt the language of the Court of Justice in the Garrido case) – then the price for the combination will be "an inclusive price" notwithstanding that it may have been calculated, arithmetically, by aggregating the prices of the components: that is to say, notwithstanding that the price for the combination is the aggregate of the prices for which each component would have been sold or offered for sale if it had been sold or offered for sale as a separate service outside the combination. The factual question to be resolved – on a case by case basis – is whether the services are being sold or offered for sale as components of a combination; or whether they are being sold or offered for sale separately, but at the same time.

27. The point may be illustrated by examples. Suppose a customer, in London, who wishes to spend a week at a named hotel in, say, Rome. He asks his travel agent what the trip will cost him. The agent ascertains that the cost of the return flight will be £X, the cost of accommodation will be £Y and the cost of the airport transfers will be £Z. Without disclosing the individual cost of each service, the agent offers the customer flights, accommodation and transfers at a price of £(X+Y+Z). The customer accepts without further inquiry. In that case there would be little doubt – as it seems to me – that the services were sold as a pre-arranged combination and at an inclusive price.

28. Now suppose that the agent has informed the customer that the cost of flights will be £X, the cost of accommodation will be

£Y and the cost of transfers will be £Z; and has explained to the customer that he can purchase any one or more of those services, as he chooses, without any need to purchase the others. He has explained, in effect, that the customer can choose to purchase the other services elsewhere; or to make other arrangements. In that case – as it seems to me – there would be little doubt that the services are not offered for sale as a pre-arranged combination and at an inclusive price.

29. What, then, if the customer chooses, and contracts for, one of those services. It is plain that that service would not be sold as a pre-arranged combination: it is not sold in combination with any other service. And it is plain that that position would not alter, if having paid for one of those services, the customer subsequently decides to take, and contracts for, another of the services. Nor would the position alter if, after paying for the second service, the customer later decides to take, and contracts for, the third service. And it would make no difference if, having entered into three separate contracts and received three separate invoices, the customer were to pay the three invoices with a single cheque. The position would be the same. There would have been no sale of a pre-arranged combination of components at a single inclusive price. Rather, there would have been three separate sales of independent services, the aggregate of the prices payable for the three separate services being satisfied by a single payment.

30. Nothing in the preceding paragraph is inconsistent with proviso (i) to the definition of "package" in the Package Travel Regulations or the ATOL Regulations ("the submission of separate accounts for different components shall not cause the arrangements to be other than a package") or with the proviso to the definition in the Directive ("The separate billing of various components of the same package shall not absolve the organiser or retailer from the obligations under this Directive"). As the judge explained at paragraph [158] of his judgment, if the arrangements would otherwise be a "package" ***– because the services are sold or offered for sale as components of a pre-arranged combination and at an inclusive*** *price – the substance of the arrangements is not altered by invoicing the components separately. But, if the arrangements would not otherwise be a "package" – because the services are, in fact, sold or offered for sale separately – separate billing merely reflects the substance of the arrangements. The most that could be said is that composite billing might be evidence (in the particular case) that the services had been sold as a package.*

31. Returning to the second of the examples which I have set out, difficult questions of fact are likely to arise if the customer chooses and contracts for two or more of the services on the same occasion. The principle is not in doubt. If the services are sold or offered for sale as components of a combination, there is a package: if they are sold or offered for sale separately but at the same time, there is no package. The question whether they are sold as components of a combination - or separately but at the same time - is a question of fact. That question may not be easy to resolve in the particular case"

Key Points

1. The court has to decide whether the services are being sold separately albeit at the same time, or as components of a combination.

2. There is an emphasis that the answer to whether there has been a package is a question of fact in each individual case. This is a strong point in favour of claimants as this could shift the burden of proof onto the defendant to prove it was not a package. Evidence could include composite billing or an absence of being told that the combination was available elsewhere and/or could be bought separately for the same price rather than being interlinked.

In *Titshall v Querty Travel Limited [2011] EWCA 1569* the Court provided some further guidance as follows, as to the test of whether a holiday is a package or not in circumstances in determining whether components were sold or offered for sale at an inclusive price, **it was**

necessary to answer the factual question of whether the services were being sold or offered for sale as components of a combination, or whether they were being sold or offered for sale separately, but at the same time.

The facts of the case were as follows:-

1. *"This appeal raises a question as to the proper application of The Package Travel, Package Holidays and Package Tours Regulations 1992, SI 1992 No 3288, to which I shall refer hereafter as "The Package Travel Regulations". Those Regulations were made under s.2(2) of the European Communities Act 1972 in order to give effect, in domestic legislation, to the Council Directive of 13 June 1990 on Package Travel, Package Holidays and Package Tours (90/314/EEC), to which I will refer hereafter as "the Directive".*

2. *The matter comes before the court by way of an appeal against a determination of a preliminary issue by District Judge Glover in the Dartford County Court. In brief outline the Claimant/Appellant Mr Titshall booked a holiday in Corfu through (I use a deliberately imprecise word) the Defendant/Respondent Qwerty Travel Limited, to which I shall refer hereafter as "Qwerty". Whilst staying at the Ermones Beach Hotel in 2006 he suffered serious injuries as a result, he says, of his attempt to open a sliding glass patio door which proved to be defective in its manufacture, in consequence of which the glass shattered. Qwerty says that at the time Mr Titshall and his partner, who had accompanied him on holiday, were heavily intoxicated and engaged in a row which generated a tussle, in the course of which he fell through, or kicked, or was forced through the glass pane. That aspect of the factual dispute remains to be tried and I need say no more about it.*

3. *In addition to joining issue with the Claimant's account of how he came by his injuries, Qwerty denies that it owed any obligation to Mr Titshall over and above that "commensurate with its role as*

> *retail agent for the suppliers of accommodation at the hotel". **In fact Qwerty says that Mr Titshall and his partner (but I will henceforth ignore her) entered into two separate contracts, one with First Choice for the supply of return flights between London Gatwick and Corfu on 25 September and 2 October 2006, and another with a company called "Hotels4U.com" for the supply of seven nights all inclusive accommodation between** those dates at the Ermones Beach Hotel. **Critically, Qwerty pleads at paragraph 2 of its Defence that Mr Titshall "did not purchase a package within the meaning of the 1992 Regulations from the Defendant". Although this may be pedantry, the relevant question is in fact whether Qwerty sold or offered for sale a package within the meaning of The Package Travel Regulations"***

The Court in this case, looked at the legislation and given the time and cost of calling witnesses from another jurisdiction said:-

> 6. "*Whilst consumer protection is plainly not the primary object of the Directive, save insofar as that can be equated with the achievement of a common market, it can **I think at the least be said that one purpose is to render it straightforward for a consumer to effect recovery from a single domestic source in the event that he has bought a package which involves the supply of services in a state other than that in which he is resident and when there is some failure properly to perform.***

> *7. **The parties agreed that there should be a preliminary hearing "to resolve the issue as to whether the claim arises from a package holiday and whether the Defendant was a party to the holiday contract".** Judge Roberts approved that approach and directed such a hearing. The parties apparently had in mind a desire not unnecessarily to incur the costs of calling witnesses from Greece. Whether this approach was best calculated to promote expeditious disposal of the claim may be open to question.*

The Court said the following in this case:-

> *22.* ***The key to the resolution of the factual enquiry whether the services were here offered for sale as the components of a combination or whether they were being sold or offered for sale separately – whether Mr Titshall was buying and paying for them as a whole – lies in my judgment in two features of the transaction. The first is that it is plain that no explicit suggestion was made to Mr Titshall that either the flights or the accommodation were available for separate purchase, the one without the other. The second is that the treatment of the service costs, however precisely that was dealt with in the elementary and simple breakdown, seems to me on the facts of this case at any rate to supply a clear unifying feature connecting the provision of the one service with the provision of the other.*** *The service costs, or at any rate the greater part thereof, must in some way have been presented as in part the price for putting together the package, not as the cost of some separate service, available in its own right, which would have been an incoherent suggestion. It is inherently unlikely to the point of being inconceivable that, insofar as it was presented as a free-standing cost, as the judge found that it was, it was put forward on the basis that that cost would be X if the flights alone were bought or Y if accommodation alone was bought.*
>
> *23. Whilst therefore I can see that the transaction had the potential to develop into an offer for sale and a sale of separate services, it did not develop in that way.* ***Qwerty offered a package which inevitably had component parts – it would not otherwise have been a package – but where those parts were presented for sale as a whole for an inclusive price which comprehended the cost of putting them together as well as the cost of sourcing them.*** *Mr Saxby's principal argument in refutation of this conclusion was that it was implicit in Mr Titshall being given a breakdown of the costs of the flights and of the accommodation that he could purchase the one rather than the other.* ***He submitted that the statement that Qwerty acted only as agents for third party suppliers who were then named served to reinforce that what was offered was two***

separate albeit simultaneous sales. I do not agree that these considerations, whether taken singly or in combination, are sufficient to achieve that result.** In my judgment the argument ignores the context of the Teletext advertisement, which was of a last minute get-away at an inclusive price (notwithstanding that that may apparently have been expressed as "from" whatever may have been the figure quoted). **In my view it ignores too the service costs, the greater part of which, without further breakdown or elucidation, necessarily represented the indivisible cost of making available the two component parts which made up the package.

25. It follows that in my judgment the judge was in error in characterising his findings of fact as amounting to Mr Titshall purchasing two services at the same time but separately. He did not purchase them separately. They were sold to him as the component parts of the combination or package. The judge's further finding that the price was not an inclusive price was, I think, simply the corollary of his conclusion that there had been two separate purchases. But in any any rate the greater part thereof. There is no principled basis upon which one can conclude that any particular proportion of the service costs should be attributed to the sale of the flights or to the sale of the accommodation, and thus whilst the sale of two services may have been identified, there is no way of ascertaining what is the total cost of either of them.

Key Points

1. The absence of an explicit suggestion that either the flights or the accommodation are available separately will present a difficulty for the defendant.

2. A separate breakdown of the components does not imply separate albeit simultaneous sales.

3. Even the defendant stating that it is acting as agent for third party suppliers and naming those does not necessarily prevent the com-

bination being a package – the context of the advertising and booking process is key. The absence of these features will clearly help the claimant's cause but this area is very complex and requires experience and judgment that would usually be best obtained by instructing specialist Counsel.

4. In a recent case dealt with by one author against a holiday company whose business was generated mostly online, the defendant company settled the claim after the telephone transcript showed that the agent had not followed the script and had not explained that the different components could be purchased separately or elsewhere. Additionally, in that case the claimant had telephoned to complete the booking because the website had stated, 'This holiday is not available online. Please telephone X Ltd'. This allowed the claimant to argue that the online terms and conditions did not apply.

5. In every case, therefore, the claimant solicitor must check for any anomaly or evidential hole in the defendant's case.

Therefore in light of *Titshall* it will be necessary to look at the following factors, if the booking was made by telephone:-

a) Were the services being sold or offered as a sale of components or a combination?

b) Was the claimant told at the time of the booking that there were a number of components to the holiday, and that these would be separate bookings?

c) Was the claimant told at the time of the booking that the Defendant was acting as agent for different companies?

d) Did the Defendant ever mention that there was another supplier of these services in the telephone conversation?

e) Did the claimant specifically request a 'holiday' booking or was the claimant seeking to book separate flights, hotels and accommodation?

It will always be necessary to try and obtain a copy of the recording of the telephone call, and/or a copy of the script that was used for the conversation by the Defendant's handling agent to see what training they were given at that time and as to what they were instructed to tell the claimant during the telephone call. In light of *Titshall* there is reasonable authority that if the separate components of the holiday were not made clear at the time of booking, i.e. during the call, when the contract is formed, it seems likely that the Court will confirm it to be a package.

Another useful authority, is in *Club-Tour v Garrido [2002] ECR 1 – 4051*. In that case the European Court of Justice was dealing with a situation where the applicant purchased a holiday from Club Tour consisting of air tickets and accommodation for two weeks at a holiday village in Greece. Club Tour purchased the holiday from a travel agency, Club Med. However, there was an infestation of wasps at the holiday village and Club Med was not able to place the customer elsewhere. He refused to pay the price of the holiday and Club Tour sought to enforce payment before the Portuguese courts.

The court was asked to answer two questions relating to the Directive, namely:

1. **Whether the word "package" in Article 2(1) of the Directive included holidays organised by a travel agency at the request of and according to the specifications of the consumer, or a defined group of consumers; and**

2. **Whether the term "pre-arranged combination" in Article 2(1) of the Directive included combinations of tourist services which were put together at the time when the contract was concluded between the travel agency and the consumer.**

The court answered both questions in the affirmative.

As to the first question, it said this:

> "***There is nothing in that definition to suggest that holidays organised at the request and in accordance with the specifications of a consumer or a defined group of consumers cannot be considered as 'package holidays'*** *within the meaning of the Directive."*

> *"As to the second question, it observed that there would still be a pre-arranged combination within the meaning of Article 2(1) even where the combination of tourist services is as a result of wishes expressed by the consumer up to the moment when the parties reach an agreement and conclude the contract. The requirement that it must pre-arranged, therefore, does not mean that it has to be a combination of services fixed by the travel agency which is made available to the consumer on a "take it or leave it" basis"*

We therefore know from this that a holiday arranged via a travel agent, can be a package for the purpose of the 1992 Regulations.

Another leading authority is *The Civil Aviation Authority v Travel Republic [2010] EWCH 1151.* The facts of this case were as follows:-

> *19.* ***TRL is a leading and highly respected British travel agent. It markets and sells to consumers air flights, hotel or other accommodation, transfers to and from airports, parking facilities, car hire, insurance and so forth.*** *It usually acts as an agent on behalf of the sellers of these services, although sometimes it is an agent of the customer.*

> *20. In effect it operates as a web search engine which facilitates a booking of travel related services.* ***It does not have brochures, it does not itself supply any services other than as an agent, and it does not have a stock of products. It takes business both from over the internet and by telephone. Typically, it will be accessed***

on the internet either directly through its own website or by following up links on a major search engine such as Google.

21. Once on the website, a customer is offered a choice of flights, hotels and apartments, car hire and other related services. Some web links specifically refer to what are described as "tailor made holidays". ***The various components which make up a holiday are ostensibly all sold separately but they can be linked together by a customer to provide all the necessary elements of a holiday, and indeed the system consciously facilitates their ability to do this. The total cost of the combined services will be the same as the aggregate cost of each component priced separately. In other words there is no price discount for booking more than one element of the holiday.***

22. A similar approach is adopted with respect to those who seek to book by telephone. ***There is a script that TRL has which is supposed to emphasise that TRL acts as agent for the providers of each component; that each component is provided separately;*** *and that TRL does not provide package holidays itself. Not surprisingly, the judge found on the evidence that in practice different telephone operatives dealt with the customer in different ways and the script is not always adopted. However, for the purposes of determining the legality of the arrangements in what is a test case, I think that we, like the judge below, must assume that the criminal liability must be the same whether the internet or telephone routes are adopted.*

23. The key issue in this case is whether by making available the flight accommodation together with some other service or services which the customer chooses to combine with it as part of a holiday, TRL was offering for sale a "pre-arranged combination of ... components ... at an inclusive price" so as to constitute a package under the Regulations. If TRL was thereby offering a package as described, it was acting unlawfully and in breach of regulation 3(1A) in providing different suppliers for different elements of the package. Save with respect to the flight element, the customers would not have any ATOL protection at all for the other elements of the holiday.

24. The submissions before the judge were essentially the same as those advanced before us. Putting it very succinctly, the CAA alleged that TRL was making available a package within the meaning of the Regulations; the situation was akin to that envisaged in the Garrido case. ***The customer is simply putting together a combination made available by the agent; to all intents and purposes the parties are agreeing a package by the time of sale.***

25. Furthermore, the CAA submitted that the construction it relies upon was supported by the decision of the Court of Appeal in The Association of British Travel Agents v The Civil Aviation Authority [2006] EWCA Civ 1356 in a judgment given by Chadwick LJ (with whose judgment Arden LJ and the President of the Family Division agreed). The component elements of the holiday were part of a linked combination for which a single inclusive price was paid.

26. TRL submitted that the judgment of Chadwick LJ in the ABTA case supported its analysis. It was not offering for sale or selling the various components of the holiday as part of a package, but merely as separate services being offered for sale at the same time. It charged a single price for such services as the customer selected but that was because it would be a pointless formality to require each service to be bought as a separate transaction requiring a separate payment.

27. The district judge found for TRL. He expressed his conclusion at [48] as follows:

"In my judgment the prosecution has failed to discharge the burden of proving that TRL did anything other than sell or offer to sell components of holidays separately, but at the same time, I am not satisfied, beyond reasonable doubt, that TRL made available to any of the customers named in the charges, flight

accommodation which constituted a component of a package holiday."

The Court in this case, went onto consider the test as to whether it was a package or not within the meaning of the 1992 Regulations:-

46. "*The issue is not whether the customer is seeking a holiday, nor even whether he would consider himself to be buying a holiday; nor is it whether a holiday is properly described as a package.* ***The issue is whether what is being made available are components of a pre- arranged combination or are separate elements being sold at the same time. Linkage between the elements is neither necessary nor sufficient to amount to a package.***

47. The judge was faced with an issue of fact to determine and he found in favour of TRL. Looking at the primary facts he was not willing to infer that this involved making available the components of a combination for an inclusive price. This was obviously not a perverse conclusion. On the contrary, it was a conclusion which was virtually dictated by paragraph 28 of Chadwick LJ's judgment. Even if that is not so, it was certainly a permissible conclusion compatible with what Chadwick LJ said in, for example, paragraph 31. As to Chadwick LJ's observation in paragraph 49 of his judgment, ***that was not envisaging a situation where the customer could select one or more services as a matter of his own choice, but rather was assuming that the agent was choosing and providing the selection for the customer.*** *In those circumstances it is easy to see why the arrangement would constitute a package as defined."*

The *Travel Republic case* was essentially concerned with a situation where the customer chose their own combination of services from a wide range of options in circumstances where the travel agent did not know whether a customer would select only a single service or a combination, or whether the customer was therefore putting together their own combination for themselves.

Key Points

1. The test is not whether a 'holiday' must inevitably mean a 'package' of different components such as flights and accommodation nor whether the customer was seeking a 'holiday' or even that he thought he was buying a 'holiday'. The subjective perception of the customer is still important, however, in resolving the relevant questions of fact and will probably bite if the agent is the one who puts together the combination rather than the customer doing so. This is more likely where the 'holiday' is arranged over the telephone or face to face rather than over the internet of course.

2. The test remains as set out by Chadwick LJ in the ABTA case: i.e. Whether what is being made available are components of a pre-arranged combination or are separate elements being sold at the same time and this is a question of fact. Persuasive advocacy will be required, however, in relation to the meaning and scope of paragraph 49 of Chadwick LJ's judgment in the *ABTA* case, if the facts suggest that the customer was putting his own package together rather than a combination suggested by the travel agent.

Conclusions

These cases are very much of assistance when dealing with bookings made over the telephone or face to face. Some points to consider may be as follows:-

a) Do you need a preliminary issue hearing on whether it is a package or not?

b) Was the holiday offered as a package at the time of booking? i.e. was the claimant told that the booking would be with separate contracts, contractors or suppliers? Was the claimant told of the separate prices for each? This will often be a question of fact and degree.

c) For telephone or face to face bookings – you will always need to obtain a copy of the transcript for a telephone booking, the script used by the agent and any booking documents either handed to the claimant at the time of booking or signed at the time. However, if the defendant is relying on a script it will be for the defendant to prove that the script was adhered to. The case law referred to above shows that the courts recognise that this is not always done.

d) A careful statement needs to be taken from the claimant if there is a dispute as to what happened during the face to face meeting or telephone call at the time of booking and whether the claimant was told about the nature of the booking and the contracts. For example, did the claimant request a package of flights, hotels, meals etc. or did the claimant approach the tour operator and ask to book flights and accommodation separately? It will help a claim if the agent made suggestions as to what hotel within a resort should be chosen.

The Package Travel, Package Holidays and Package Tours Regulations 1992 – What is a Package? – Website Bookings

In the *Civil Aviation v Travel Republic Limited case [2010] EWHC 1151* the Court said as follows with regards to website bookings:-

19. "In effect it operates as a web search engine which facilitates a booking of travel related services. It does not have brochures, it does not itself supply any services other than as an agent, and it does not have a stock of products. It takes business both from over the internet and by telephone. Typically, it will be accessed on the internet either directly through its own website or by following up links on a major search engine such as Google.

20. Once on the website, a customer is offered a choice of flights, hotels and apartments, car hire and other related services. Some web links specifically refer to what are described as

> ***"tailor made holidays". The various components which make up a holiday are ostensibly all sold separately but they can be linked together by a customer to provide all the necessary elements of a holiday, and indeed the system consciously facilitates their ability to do this. The total cost of the combined services will be the same as the aggregate cost of each component priced separately. In other words there is no price discount for booking more than one element of the holiday"***

In other words, the test will be whether the individual components of the holiday were purchased separately, i.e. the consumer selecting various components in one basket and paying for them at the same time, identified as separate components or whether as in the case above *"If the services are sold or offered for sale as components of a combination, there is a package: if they are sold or offered for sale separately but at the same time, there is no package. The question whether they are sold as components of a combination - or separately but at the same time - is a question of fact. That question may not be easy to resolve in the particular case".*

On a website booking case it will be necessary to establish the following:-

1. What did the website look like, at the time the booking was made – not months or years later when the claim is made?

2. How were the components of the holiday booked? Did the claimant choose a flights and hotel separately, i.e. as different components or were the matters offered as one price?

3. If the website purports to have a disclaimer that the contracts are with separate parties, can the defendant provide evidence this was in place at the time of the booking and how would this have been visible to the consumer?

It will therefore be necessary to seek disclosure of the following documents from the defendant:-

a) Screenshots of how the booking system looked at when the booking was made, including screen shots of any alleged disclaimer.

b) Details of the defendant's website updates and copies of how the booking terms and screens have been amended since the booking was made. The Defendant is likely to keep a log of website updates.

c) Screenshots of how the holiday purchase screen would have looked to the consumer when the booking was made and details of the defendant's website updates and copies of how the booking terms and screens have been amended since the booking was made.

As in *Gallagher v Airtours Holidays [2001] CLY 480* makes it clear that the transparency of the booking is key – how clear would it have been that the consumer would have been aware the booking was being made by separate retailers?

However in order for the holiday booked via a website to be a package it must be '*pre arranged and the combination must be offered or sold at an inclusive price*'. The *ABTA v CAA* cases said:-

> *"18. The requirement that the components of the package must be sold or offered for sale as a "pre-arranged combination" is met not only where the components are put together by the organiser without input from the customer (typically, the brochure holiday) but also where the components are put together by the organiser in accordance with the specifications of the individual customer (or consumer) or group of customers (typically, the 'customised' holiday) – Club-Tour, Viagrens e Turismo SA v Alberto Carlos Lobo GonÇalves Garrido (Case C-400/00) [2002] ECR I-4051. And the requirement is satisfied not only in cases where the components have been put together and offered for sale by the organiser in advance of any contact with the individual customer but also in cases "where the combination of tourist services is the result of the wishes*

expressed by the customer up to the moment when the parties reach an agreement and conclude the contract" – ibid, paragraph [19]. It can be seen, of course, that the principle is expressly stated, as proviso (ii), in the definition of "package" in both the Package Travel Regulations and the ATOL Regulations (as amended in 2003). That proviso did not appear in the Directive, which was the text which the Court of Justice was required to consider in the Garrido case."

Conclusions

It may be argued that where various components are offered for sale on a single website, the contract will likely be pre-arranged. However, where the holiday components are purchased from different websites or, the main website provides links to different websites to make the purchases of different components, i.e. for flights and hotels, it is unlikely that this will be held to be a package, as it would not be pre-arranged at an all inclusive price.

Key Point

As with most litigation, but particularly in relation to website bookings, it is essential to have a focussed Reply to Defence that puts the defendant to strict proof in relation to the evidential matters referred to above. A carefully drafted Reply can cause fatal problems for a defendant later including at trial if they have failed to provide or even seek this evidence.

CHAPTER TWO
CLAIMS UNDER THE ATHENS CONVENTION FOR ACCIDENTS AT SEA AND CRUISE SHIP CLAIMS

The Athens Convention deals with accidents on board ships. Accidents on board ships can range from food poisoning to slips, trips and falls. The claim could be brought against a cruise ship, ferry, pleasure craft or yacht. To bring a claim under the convention, the claim must include a stop off in a country outside the UK, it does not apply to solely domestic cruises.

The original Athens Convention was originally implemented into English Law by the Merchant Shipping Act 1995. From 31 December 2012 Regulation EC 392/2009 of the European Parliament and the Council on the liability of carriers of passengers by sea in the events of accidents (the 2009 Regulations) applies. These are supplemented by the Merchant Shipping (Carriage of Passengers by Sea) Regulations 2012. The 2009 Regulations adopt the 2002 Protocol. The consolidated convention will apply to claims after 31 December 2012. The relevant Regulations are reproduced in Schedule 6 of the Merchant Shipping Act 1995.

The relevant sections set out liability to the carrier as follows:-

Article 14

Basis for claims

No action for damages for the death of or personal injury to a passenger, or for the loss of or damage to luggage, shall be brought against a carrier or performing carrier otherwise than in accordance with this Convention.

Article 17
Competent jurisdiction

An action arising under this Convention shall, at the option of the claimant, be brought before one of the courts listed below, provided that the court is located in a State Party to this Convention:

(a) the court of the place of permanent residence or principal place of business of the defendant, or

(b) the court of the place of departure or that of the destination according to the contract of carriage, or

(c) a court of the State of the domicile or permanent residence of the claimant, if the defendant has a place of business and is subject to jurisdiction in that State, or

(d) a court of the State where the contract of carriage was made, if the defendant has a place of business and is subject to jurisdiction in that State.

2 After the occurrence of the incident which has caused the damage, the parties may agree that the claim for damages shall be submitted to any jurisdiction or to arbitration.

One of the first matters to look at is whether the English Court has jurisdiction under the convention to hear the claim. Thus according to Article 17, as long as the Defendant is based in England and Wales, where the contract was made, the claimant will be able to bring a claim under the convention in England and Wales.

One of the other key issues to consider in these types of claim is that of limitation. The convention says:-

Article 16

Time-bar for actions

1 Any action for damages arising out of the death of or personal injury to a passenger or for the loss of or damage to luggage shall be time-barred after a period of two years.

2 The limitation period shall be calculated as follows:

(a) in the case of personal injury, from the date of disembarkation of the passenger;

(b) in the case of death occurring during carriage, from the date when the passenger should have disembarked, and in the case of personal injury occurring during carriage and resulting in the death of the passenger after disembarkation, from the date of death, provided that this period shall not exceed three years from the date of disembarkation;

(c) in the case of loss of or damage to luggage, from the date of disembarkation or from the date when disembarkation should have taken place, whichever is later.

3 The law of the court seized of the case shall govern the grounds of suspension and interruption of limitation periods, but in no case shall an action under this Convention be brought after the expiration of a period of three years from the date of disembarkation of the passenger or from the date when disembarkation should have taken place, whichever is later.

4 Notwithstanding paragraphs 1, 2 and 3 of this Article, the period of limitation may be extended by a declaration of the carrier or by agreement of the parties after the cause of action has arisen. The declaration or agreement shall be in writing.

In the very sad instance where the claimant is likely to die or could do soon, the claim must be issued before the end of the 3-year limitation period.

In Athens conventions claims proceedings must be commenced inside the two year period, and section 33 of the Limitation Act 1980, will arguably not assist in such cases.

One must be careful to ensure in these types of claims that the parties to the proceedings will fall inside the definitions of those applicable to the legislation:-

Article 1

Definitions

In this Convention the following expressions have the meaning hereby assigned to them:

1 (a) "carrier" means a person by or on behalf of whom a contract of carriage has been concluded, whether the carriage is actually performed by him or by a performing carrier;

(b) "performing carrier" means a person other than the carrier, being the owner, charterer or operator of a ship, who actually performs the whole or a part of the carriage;

2 "contract of carriage" means a contract made by or on behalf of a carrier for the carriage by sea of a passenger or of a passenger and his luggage, as the case may be;

3 "ship" means only a seagoing vessel, excluding an air-cushion vehicle;

4 "passenger" means any person carried in a ship,

(a) under a contract of carriage, or

(b) who, with the consent of the carrier, is accompanying a vehicle or live animals which are covered by a contract for the carriage of goods not governed by this Convention;

Liability is defined under the *2002 Protocol to the Athens Convention relating to the Carriage of Passengers and their Luggage by Sea, 1974* as follows:-

ARTICLE 4

Liability of the carrier

Article 3 of the Convention is replaced by the following text:

Article 3

1 For the loss suffered as a result of the death of or personal injury to a passenger caused by a shipping incident, the carrier shall be liable to the extent that such loss in respect of that passenger on each distinct occasion does not exceed 250,000 units of account, unless the carrier proves that the incident:

(a) resulted from an act of war, hostilities, civil war, insurrection or a natural phenomenon of an exceptional, inevitable and irresistible character; or

(b) was wholly caused by an act or omission done with the intent to cause the incident by a third party. If and to the extent that the loss exceeds the above limit, the carrier shall be further liable unless the carrier proves that the incident which caused the loss occurred without the fault or neglect of the carrier.

2 For the loss suffered as a result of the death of or personal injury to a passenger not caused by a shipping incident, the carrier shall be liable if the incident which caused the loss was due to the fault or neglect of the carrier. The burden of proving fault or neglect shall lie with the claimant.

3 For the loss suffered as a result of the loss of or damage to cabin luggage, the carrier shall be liable if the incident which caused the loss was due to the fault or neglect of the carrier. The fault or neglect of the carrier shall be presumed for loss caused by a shipping incident.

4 For the loss suffered as a result of the loss of or damage to luggage other than cabin luggage, the carrier shall be liable unless the carrier proves that the incident which caused the loss occurred without the fault or neglect of the carrier.

5 For the purposes of this Article:

(a) shipping incident. means shipwreck, capsizing, collision or stranding of the ship, explosion or fire in the ship, or defect in the ship;

(b) fault or neglect of the carrier. includes the fault or neglect of the servants of the carrier, acting within the scope of their employment;

(c) defect in the ship. means any malfunction, failure or non-compliance with applicable safety regulations in respect of any part of the ship or its equipment when used for the escape, evacuation, embarkation and disembarkation of passengers; or when used for the propulsion, steering, safe navigation, mooring, anchoring, arriving at or leaving berth or anchorage, or damage control after flooding; or when used for the launching of life saving appliances; and

(d) loss. shall not include punitive or exemplary damages.
The liability of the carrier under this Article only relates to loss arising from

6 incidents that occurred in the course of the carriage. The burden of proving that the incident which caused the loss occurred in the course of the carriage, and the extent of the loss, shall lie with the claimant.

7 Nothing in this Convention shall prejudice any right of recourse of the carrier against any third party, or the defence of contributory negligence under Article 6 of this Convention. Nothing in this Article shall prejudice any right of limitation under Articles 7 or 8 of this Convention.

8 Presumptions of fault or neglect of a party or the allocation of the burden of proof to a party shall not prevent evidence in favour of that party from being considered.

In such a case, the Claimant (passenger) will bear the burden of proving the fault or neglect of the carrier to the extent of the damage suffered. It is necessary in this context to look at a number of cases which provide examples of how the burden of proof has been applied in Athens Convention cases. In the case of JANET DAWKINS v CARNIVAL PLC (T/A P&O CRUISES) (2011), the facts were as follows (applying the Athens Convention 1974 tests):-

1. This is an appeal against a judgment of Mr Recorder Wright given on 3 December 2010 at Southampton County Court. The Recorder dismissed a claim by Mrs Janet Dawkins ("the appellant") for damages for personal injuries sustained by her on 23 November 2006 while a passenger in international waters on the P&O cruise ship "Oriana" operated by the respondents.

2. The claim was pleaded under the Occupiers' Liability Act 1957 but it is common ground that it was governed by the Athens Convention on Carriage of Passengers and their Luggage by Sea (1974), incorporated into the law of England and Wales by section 183 of the Merchant Shipping Act 1995. This was "international carriage" of a passenger pursuant to a contract of carriage within the Convention. Article 3(1) of the Convention provides:

"The carrier shall be liable for the damage suffered as a result of the death of or personal injury to a passenger and the loss of or damage to luggage if the incident which caused the damage so suffered occurred in the course of the carriage and was due to the fault or

neglect of the carrier or of his servants or agents acting within the scope of their employment."

Article 3(3), having dealt with situations not relevant to the present case, provides:

"In all other cases the burden of proving fault or neglect shall lie with the claimant."

3. It is accepted, for present purposes, that the tests to be applied under the Convention, including as to burden of proof, are the same as they would have been had the accident happened on premises in England and Wales. No point is taken on the defect in pleading.

4. When walking through the Conservatory Restaurant on the ship at about 2 pm, the appellant fell, sustaining soft tissue injuries to both knees and her wrists. The judge found, on balance of probabilities, that the appellant slipped "on some liquid, probably water, on the floor of the Conservatory". Staff were soon assisting her. When she slipped, the appellant was passing a drinks dispensing station. The only evidence of how long the water had been there was that of fellow passengers Mr and Mrs Thomas who said that "it was not there when they got to the Conservatory, which may have been from 10 minutes to 30 minutes before the accident". The Recorder stated, at paragraph 17, that "in theory at least, the spillage could have occurred only moments before, or several minutes before the accident."

5. The Conservatory is one of the most popular and high-traffic venues on board. It is manned throughout the day and is in constant use by passengers. The accident happened near what is known as a clearing station where someone should be "permanently present", the Recorder found.

6. The Recorder found, at paragraph 16:

"Nevertheless the possibility of spillage in the cafeteria, and of someone slipping on spilt liquid, are obviously foreseeable. Although a danger such as this could be expected or at least foreseen also by a passenger, nevertheless it obviously imposes on the Defendant a clear duty to operate a reasonably effective system for getting rid of spilt liquid, and minimising the danger it may cause. The fact that in the ordinary course of things an accident such as this would not normally happen clearly raises the suggestion that the accident arose from want of care by the Defendant. It will be for the Defendants to discharge an evidential burden to the effect that the accident did not happen through want of care on their part. In effect it is for the Defendants to show that the accident was not the result of any failure by them."

7. At paragraph 18, the Recorder stated:
". . . one could not expect a system of continual inspection of every part of the floor. There are bound to be occasions when liquid is spilt, specially in this area. . . . Thus there are bound to be times when there is unguarded spillage on the floor. ***A properly operated system must take this into account, but no system can completely prevent this."***

The Court of Appeal in Dawkins went onto look at the test to be applied in such cases – it said:-

"I approach the case in stages:

(a) The burden of proof is upon the appellant. ***At the end of the trial it is for the claimant to show on a balance of probabilities that the accident was caused by negligence on the part of the respondents.***

(b) Where premises, such as the floor of the Conservatory in this case, are under the management of defendants and a hazard is present on the floor, there may be a prima facie case of negligence

against the defendants. The strength of the case will depend on all the circumstances.

(c) In the present circumstances, there was a prima facie case, as the judge found.

(d) The issue is whether, on the evidence as a whole, that case was displaced. The respondents submitted that by calling evidence of a usually good system of inspection and observation, it was displaced.

25. For the respondents, Mr Palmer QC submitted that the Recorder was entitled to reach the conclusion he did. Though not spelt out precisely in these terms, the Recorder drew, and was entitled to draw, the inference from the evidence of a system of work that it was operating at the material time. That being so, the liquid could not have been on the floor for a significant time and the claim failed. It was not fatal to the defence that no evidence was called from those working in the Conservatory at or around the time of the accident. In the absence of evidence that the water had been on the floor for a significant period of time, the appellant had not discharged the burden on her of proving negligence, it was submitted.

26. On the face of it, the presence of the liquid was more consistent with fault on the part of the respondents than with absence of fault on their part. The area was under their close control and liquid was present on the floor.

27. I accept that if the probability is of such contemporaneity between the spillage and the accident that remedial action could not reasonably be taken during the gap between them, the claim would fail. The Recorder did not make a finding as to time but, if the defendants could demonstrate such contemporaneity, the claim would fail.

28. The absence of evidence from one or more of the many members of staff claimed to be present in the Conservatory at the material time is remarkable. The explanation for the lack of evidence from a

> *member or members of staff was, the Recorder found, that the defendants "could not establish who it was."* ***In my judgment, in the absence of evidence from members of staff claimed to be implementing the system, the judge was not entitled to infer from the existence of a system that the spillage which led to the fall occurred only a few seconds, or a very short time, before the accident.***
>
> *29. The claim succeeds on the evidence in this case. There is nothing to suggest such closeness in time between the spillage and the accident as would, at a place where close observation was required, exclude liability.* ***In the absence of evidence to the contrary, I can conclude only that on a balance of probabilities the water had been there for longer than the very brief period which, in this particular place, would have excused the defendants from taking remedial action before the accident.***
>
> *30. I would allow this appeal and remit the case to the County Court for the assessment of damages. The court has not accepted the submission on behalf of the appellant that the case must be heard by a different judge. The Recorder has heard evidence relevant to damages. However, the case can be heard by a different judge if listing requirements make that a more suitable course.".*

The case is therefore akin to that of a *Ward v Tesco* slipping scenario, that is to say if the Claimant can show prima facie evidence of negligence, i.e something on the floor that caused him to slip, it is up to the defendant, in this case the carrier to show that it had a reasonable system in place. In Dawkins, this meant that in the absence of evidence from members of staff claimed to be implementing the system, the judge was not entitled to infer from the existence of a system that the spillage which led to the claimant's fall occurred only a very short time before the accident and therefore her claim succeeded.

Another case which succeeded was ARTHUR LAWRENCE v NCL (BAHAMAS) LTD (T/A NORWEGIAN CRUISE LINE) (2016). The issues as to how these type of claims are brought in Law under the Convention was helpfully summarised as follows:-

> "*Injuries occurring onboard ships are Admiralty claims which must be commenced in the Admiralty Court by reason of the provisions* ***contained in sections 20(1) and 20(2)(f) and CPR Parts 61.1(2) (a) and 61 .2(l)(a)(v).*** *However cases which do not involve matters of maritime interest or expertise, such as cases involving injuries which might otherwise have occurred ashore including injuries arising from slipping, falling or food poisoning, may and usually are transferred to the County Court or to the Central Office of the Queen's Bench Division of the High Court depending upon the level of damages claimed and the complexity of the case. Similarly personal injury claims in which liability has been admitted, so that the only remaining issue is the assessment of the appropriate sum of damages, are generally transferred to the County Court or the Central Office of the Queen's Bench Division of the High Court.*
>
> *In the present case, although the overall level of damages was moderate (and became more modest as the opinion of experts was obtained and assessed) the Defendant has continued to deny liability for what is essentially a maritime incident and therefore the claim was retained in the Admiralty Court and was allocated for trial before myself as Admiralty Registrar*"

The facts of the case were as follows:-

> *In the Claim Form and its attached Particulars of Claim it is alleged that:*
>
> ***a. The Defendant was the carrier and or performing carrier within the provisions of Art. 1 of the Athens Convention 1974*** *(enacted by s.l83 of the Merchant Shipping Act 1995).*
>
> *b. The Convention applied to the carriage of the Claimant onboard the ship because:*

i. It was incorporated by the standard booking terms and conditions of the contract, and;

ii. The cruise was international carriage within the meaning of Art. 1(9) of the Athens Convention;

3

iii. The contract of carriage was entered into in the United Kingdom which is state party to the Athens Convention Within the meaning of Art. 2(1) of the Athens Convention.

c. The Defendant offered shore excursions one of which was at Santorini on the 2"' July 2014 by way of tender.

cl. The Claimant and his wife boarded the tender. The upper deck was full, the lower deck was dark and unlit and the deck was painted black. There were no members of staff to assist the passengers.

e. As the Claimant walked forward he tripped over an isolated step which caused him to be injured.

f. The incident and the injuries were caused by the fault of the Defendant. The main failings alleged were, stated briefly:

i. In failing to warn of the step, highlight it, adequately light it;
ii. In failing to have a safe or adequate system for boarding the passengers;
iii. Used a tender with an unsafe step on the deck.

g. The alleged injury sustained was a tear to the supraspinatus within the rotator cuff of the left shoulder restricting movement of the shoulder"

The Defendant replied:-

"In its Defence NCL contends that:

i The injury did not occur on the Ship;

b. NCL was not the carrier or performing carrier within the meaning of Art. 1 of the Athens Convention;

c. The contract of carriage onboard the Ship was made between the Claimant and Flight and Packages Ltd;

d. The Defendant did not own or operate and has no control over the tender. The carriage onboard the tender was not a period of carriage within the meaning of para. 8(a) of Art. 1 of the Athens Convention;

e. No admissions are made and the Claimant should be put to proof of its contract with Flights and Packages Ltd and as to how and when it was concluded;

ii. as to whether an excursion was offered;

iii. as to the description of the tender, how he was injured and matters relating to the "step";

iv. as to the injuries suffered and whether they arose from the incident"

The Court found in favour of the Claimant and applied the principles under the 1974 Convention as follows: -

"*Consideration*

14. The disputed issues between the parties were in essence as follows:

Application of the Athens Convention:

> *Whether the Defendant was the carrier or the performing carrier (or both) in respect of the cruise.*
>
> *Whether the incident on the tender boat occurred in the course of carriage.*
>
> *Whether the incident was caused by the fault or neglect of the Defendant or its servants or agents acting within the scope of their employment (Article 3(1) and Article 4(1)).*

On the issues the Court made the following findings.

The Court found that the documents showed the Claimant was the 'carrier' for the purpose of the convention and that it was clear that the carriage included periods while the passenger was in the course of disembarkation and the period while he was being transported from the ship to the land and vice versa. They key issue was the interpretation of the fault based system under the convention and the Court said, finding for the Claimant:-

> "*To establish liability the Claimant needed to show that his injury was caused by either the carrier or by performing carrier for whose acts the carrier is liable......*
>
> *The carriers are bound to take reasonable care of their passengers. The fact is that the vast majority of cruise passengers are retired people and therefore, by reason of age, less able to look after themselves than younger more able bodied persons. It follows that cruise operators and any performing carriers should take it upon themselves to exercise that care which is commensurate with carrying elderly passengers who might be less wary of potential danger*"

Therefore in the instant case, this is a helpful example of how the Court imposed a duty of a standard akin to the standard common law duty of care and adapting the systems for health and safety according to the persons on board the ship. The Court found the sill was a hazard and found that it had not been marked, there was nothing to warn passengers of the danger and once there was a hazard the defendant should have arranged for appropriate steps to be taken, once the hazard was identified.

CHAPTER THREE
AIR ACCIDENTS AND THE MONTREAL CONVENTION

The Montreal Convention deals with air accidents or personal injury on board aircraft. It came into force in June 2004. The Convention (Montreal Convention on International Carriage by Air 1999) sets out as follows:-

Article 1 – Scope of application

1. This Convention applies to all international carriage of persons, baggage or cargo performed by aircraft for reward. It applies equally to gratuitous carriage by aircraft performed by an air transport undertaking.

2. For the purposes of this Convention, the expression "international carriage" means any carriage in which, according to the agreement between the parties, the place of departure and the place of destination, whether or not there be a break in the carriage or a transhipment, are situated either within the territories of two States Parties, or within the territory of a single State Party if there is an agreed stopping place within the territory of another State, even if that State is not a State Party. Carriage between two points within the territory of a single State Party without an agreed stopping place within the territory of another State is not international carriage for the purposes of this Convention.

3. Carriage to be performed by several successive carriers is deemed, for the purposes of this Convention, to be one undivided carriage if it has been regarded by the parties as a single operation, whether it had been agreed upon under the form of a single contract or of a series of contracts, and it does not lose its interna-

tional character merely because one contract or a series of contracts is to be performed entirely within the territory of the same State.

4. This Convention applies also to carriage as set out in Chapter V, subject to the terms contained therein.

In order for there to be a claim under the convention, there has to be 'an agreement for carriage', that it to say the airline agrees to transport the passenger as per paragraph 2 above but if there is more than one carrier, the carrier is liable for the section of the journey it has reasonability for.

In respect of a claim for personal injury, Article 17 sets out as follows:-

Article 17 – Death and injury of passengers – damage to baggage

1. The carrier is liable for damage sustained in case of death or bodily injury of a passenger upon condition only that the accident which caused the death or injury took place on board the aircraft or in the course of any of the operations of embarking or disembarking.

2. The carrier liable for damage sustained in case of destruction or loss of, or of damage to, checked baggage upon condition only that the event which caused the destruction, loss or damage took place on board the aircraft or during any period within which the checked baggage was in the charge of the carrier. However, the carrier is not liable if and to the extent that the damage resulted from the inherent defect, quality or vice of the baggage. In the case of unchecked baggage, including personal items, the carrier is liable if the damage resulted from its fault or that of its servants or agents.

3. If the carrier admits the loss of the checked baggage, or if the checked baggage has not arrived at the expiration of twenty-one days after the date on which it ought to have arrived, the passenger is entitled to enforce against the carrier the rights which flow from the contract of carriage.

4. Unless otherwise specified, in this Convention the term "baggage" means both checked baggage and unchecked baggage.

An accident could include an air crash, collision on the runway, a collapsing seat, a defective seat, spilling of hot food or drink, food poisoning, or falling items from lockers. An accident would probably not cover an injury caused by deceleration on landing, DVT or a perforated eardrum caused by normal decompression. The following cases may assist in terms of establishing breach of duty:-

In ANNE FORD v MALAYSIAN AIRLINE SYSTEMS BERHAD (2013), the Court helped to define the meaning of an accident. The Court held that the act of giving an air passenger an injection of a diuretic in the course of an international commercial flight, which exacerbated her physical discomfort caused by fluid retention resulting from urethral stenosis, did not constitute an "accident" for the purposes of the Montreal Convention on International Carriage by Air 1999 art.17.1. The Court said the key question was therefore whether the actual act of giving F an injection of a diuretic in the circumstances that prevailed could be characterised as an unusual event from F's perspective and whether the "unusual nature" of that event was a "cause" leading to the bodily injury. The circumstances in which the injection was administered by D could not be characterised as "unusual" for the purposes of art.17.1. There was no evidence that the administration of the injection was done in an abnormal way. The only unusual aspect of the injection was that it was carried out in the course of an international flight by a passenger doctor on another passenger, with proper consent, as a result of a request to the doctor for assistance by a crew member. There was no evidence that any of those characteristics had any causative effect in the chain of events that led to F's bodily injury. The same chain of events would have taken place wherever the injection had been administered. The simple fact that the injection was administered in mid-flight rather than elsewhere could not provide the circumstances with the necessary unusual characteristics so that the event constituted an accident within art.17.1.

In BUCKLEY v MONARCH AIRLINES LTD (2012), a claimant established that she had suffered a bodily injury whilst on board an aircraft and that the incident was an unusual and unexpected event, but failed to prove that her injury had been caused by an "accident" which had happened independently of anything done by her. The Court found the claimant did not have to prove negligence. However, the Court said that to establish breach the claimant had to establish (a) that there had been "an unexpected or unusual event", and (b) that it was "external", in the sense that it had not been caused or contributed to by her. This case involved a spillage of hot water but the case failed as there was no evidence to suggest that the spillage had been caused by the expected operation of the aircraft and the claimant's assertion that she hadn't touched the cup was rejected.

In BEVERLEY ANNE BARCLAY v BRITISH AIRWAYS PLC (2008), this was another case that looked at the same point. It said the Montreal Convention on International Carriage by Air 1999 art.17 contemplated, by the term "accident", a distinct event, not being any part of the usual, normal and expected operation of the aircraft, which happened independently of anything done or omitted by the passenger. The Judgment set out:-

> "***The appellant's claim could only prevail if it fell within the terms of Article 17.1 of the Montreal Convention 1999, which provides:***

"The carrier is liable for damage sustained in case of death or bodily injury of a passenger upon condition only that the accident which caused the death or injury took place on board the aircraft or in the course of any of the operations of embarking or disembarking."

Article 17.1 has the force of law in England by virtue of Schedule 1B to the Carriage by Air Act 1961. It provides an exclusive remedy: Sidhu v British Airways plc [1997] AC 430, El Al Airlines Ltd v Tseng (1999) 525 US 155. *Its predecessor was Article 17 of the Warsaw Convention 1929 as amended, whose terms were in material respects to the same effect as those of Article 17.1 of the Montreal Convention. I should note, however, that the Warsaw Convention was concluded in French. An English translation appeared in the Carriage by Air Act 1932, which gave the Convention the force of law in England. The result was that in relation to international carriage by air, the French text was to prevail in the case of difference. The Montreal Convention, however, was drafted in English.*

The question in this case was, and is, whether the injuries sustained by the claimant were caused by an accident within the meaning of Article 17.1"

By common consent the leading case on Article 17 of the Warsaw Convention, no less applicable to Article 17.1, is ***Air France v Saks (1985) 470 US 392 in the United States Supreme Court****. The claimant, a passenger aboard an aircraft coming in to land, suffered pressure and pain in her left ear and was later diagnosed permanently deaf in that ear. The aircraft's pressurisation system was working normally. The airline moved for summary judgment against the claimant on the ground that she could not prove that* *her injury had been caused by an "accident" within Article 17 of the Warsaw Convention.*

O'Connor J, delivering the opinion of the Supreme Court, analysed the text of the Convention (in both languages), the negotiating history of the Convention and the travaux preparatories, along with existing authority of courts in the United States and elsewhere. She identified two "clues", as she described them, to the meaning of the term "accident". The first was the contrast between the word "accident" in Article 17 and "occurrence" in Article 18 (dealing with liability for the destruction or loss of baggage) - "accident" thus means something different from "occurrence". (I should say that Article 18.1 of the Montreal Convention has the word "event" in place of "occurrence", but the force of the contrast, I think, remains the same). The second clue was that Article 17 refers to an accident which caused the passenger's injury, not an accident which was the passenger's injury. So the accident and the injury are clearly separated.

At length O'Connor J stated at p. 405:

"We conclude that liability under Article 17 of the Warsaw Convention arises only if a passenger's injury is caused by an unexpected or unusual event or happening that is external to the passenger. This definition should be flexibly applied after assessment of all the circumstances surrounding a passenger's injuries."

She added at p. 406:

"... [W]hen the injury indisputably results from the passenger's own internal reaction to the usual, normal, and expected oper-

ation of the aircraft, it has not been caused by an accident, and Article 17 of the Warsaw Convention cannot apply."

The Court helpfully outlined various scenarios as to the definition of injury:-

> 10.*It is convenient at this stage to identify precisely the issue we have to decide. As I have indicated, the appellant must show that her injuries were caused by an accident within the meaning of Article 17.1.* ***Thus the scope of the term "accident" is critical. It is clear (I shall cite relevant authority shortly) that proof of fault on the part of the carrier*** *is not required. But "accident" cannot mean any occurrence on the aircraft which causes injury. So much at least is clear from Saks. To elucidate its scope in a thumbnail sketch, we may postulate three situations. (1)* ***A member of the cabin staff loses his footing in the gangway and spills hot coffee, burning a passenger's hand. Plainly there is an accident; in the language of the Saks decision, "an unexpected or unusual event or happening that is external to the passenger". (2) A passenger suffers a heart attack unprompted by any event in the aircraft. As Mr Menzies accepted, plainly there is no accident; there is no event which might qualify as such****. This situation is not far from the actual facts in Chaudhari (unreported: transcript 16 April 1997, Court of Appeal), to which I will refer. (3) The third situation is this present case. On the one hand, there is no event entirely unconnected with the passenger, such as the crew member losing his footing in situation (1). On the other, the injury is not caused by an autonomous collapse in the passenger's health with which the aircraft environment had nothing to do, as in situation (2). Mr Menzies' case is that there was an accident causative of his client's injury – her slipping on the plastic strip. Mr Lawson for the respondent submits by contrast that there was no accident –*

the slip was not an untoward event external to the passenger: the plastic strip was inert in its ordinary condition; nothing happened save for the appellant's coming into contact with it. *The issue in the appeal can accordingly be stated in this way: where injury is caused by an event (here the slip) constituted by some contact or interaction between the passenger and the aeroplane in its normal state, is such an event an "accident" within Article 17.1?*

15.***In DVT and Air Travel Group Litigation [2006]*** *1 AC 495 Lord Scott of Foscote described the canons of construction applicable to Article 17 of the earlier Convention in a passage which also reflects the balance of interests which the Convention strikes:*

"11. Counsel for the parties were in broad agreement as to the principles of interpretation of article 17 that should be applied. The important principles for present purposes are that:

(1) **the starting point is to consider the natural meaning of the language of article 17 ...;**

(2) the Convention should be considered as a whole and given a purposive interpretation;

(3) the language of the Convention should not be interpreted by reference to domestic law principles or domestic rules of interpretation; and

(4) assistance can and should be sought from relevant decisions of the courts of other Convention countries, but the weight to be given to them will depend upon the standing of the court concerned and the quality of the analysis. ***I would add to these that the balance***

struck by the Convention between the interests of passengers and the interest of the airlines ought not to be distorted by a judicial approach to interpretation in a particular case designed to reflect the merits of that case."

"23. One can break down the definition of an accident into two elements. (1) There must be an event; (2) the event must be unusual, unexpected or untoward. I would endorse the approval by the United States Court of Appeals, ***Third Circuit in Abramson v Japan Airlines Co Ltd (1984) 739 F 2d 130, 132, of the following charge to a jury as to the correct legal standard for determining the occurrence of an accident under Article 17:***

'An accident is an event, a physical circumstance, which unexpectedly takes place not according to the usual course of things. If the event on board an airplane is an ordinary, expected, and usual occurrence, then it cannot be termed an accident. To constitute an accident, the occurrence on board the aircraft must be unusual or unexpected, an unusual or unexpected happening.'"

It is clear from the concurring judgments of Judge LJ (as he then was) and Kay LJ that they too regarded the reasoning in Saks as an uncontentious premise of the debate.

Lord Steyn, after citing Saks, said:

"33. ***Let it be assumed that it can be shown that an event affecting a passenger adversely on an aircraft was unexpected and unusual. That is generally, however, not enough to make it an accident. It is an integral part of the test of what amounts to an accident that it must have a cause external to the passenger.*** *In the case of DVT this factor is absent. The component parts of the event cannot therefore amount to an accident.* ***It is closer to a pas-***

senger who suffers an asthmatic attack, congenital back pain, a hiatus hernia or simply from the wear and tear of extreme old age. Not surprisingly, such cases have in practice been treated as not amounting to accidents*: see Shawcross and Beaumont, Air Law, VII, para 701 (Shawcross Issue 101). Consequentialist arguments militate in favour of treating essentially similar medical cases in the same legal way. After all, DVT is not immune from the general process of medical science."*

As an example of another case that succeed on appeal DARSHAN SINGHAL v BRITISH AIRWAYS PLC (2007), initially failed where the claimant had sustained an ankle injury as a result of an accident within the meaning of the Montreal Convention on International Carriage by Air 1999 art.17 where the jetway used by passengers to disembark from an aircraft had been aligned below the bottom of the aircraft door creating an unexpected step, which caused the appellant to lose her footing and fall. The Court said on Appeal:-

"***Reasons for holding that Appellant suffered Article 17 accident***

38.*In my view, this conclusion cannot be supported.* ***Whilst I accept, as was made clear in the Court of Appeal by Lord Phillips in DVT, (para. 63) that a failure to warn of a potential risk could not of itself constitute an accident under Article 17, the plain fact is that there was a step of which the Appellant, who had just completed a 7 hour transatlantic flight was quite reasonably unaware, and the fall resulting from this step was clearly the result of a factor which was external to her. These were consequences which were both "unintended" and "unexpected" from her viewpoint. The District Judge's findings that the positioning of the jetway resulting in an unexpected 6 inch step, albeit in conformity with the particular requirements of the manual in use at Heathrow Airport, was one which was***

not unusual or untoward "even for a passenger in Mrs Singhal's position" and that the cause of the fall "was not an untoward occurrence" are, in my view, factually and legally unsupportable. *I am quite unable to accept that a unexpected and unforeseen six inch step is not to be regarded as "untoward" in the context of exiting procedures from a passenger aircraft"*

43. *The Convention is an international one and should be interpreted, so far as practicable, in the same manner in all the subscribing jurisdictions. Thus, in the absence of proper evidence, I would regard it as dangerous to make a finding which is confined to the apparent practice at Heathrow Airport – of which, incidentally, I was provided with only scant details. There is, for example, no evidence whatever of the practice at other airports, whether in the UK or elsewhere, with regard to Boeing 777 aircraft or other aircraft with different exit characteristics, whether this form of alignment is universal, whether different types of jetway are used which eliminate the necessity for a step, whether ramps are employed, whether practices elsewhere are to give warnings, – and so and so forth. It would thus be unsafe to make a finding which is based only on the manual in use at Heathrow Airport, especially as the uncontradicted evidence of the Appellant was that no such step was present on a Virgin aircraft on which she flew.*

44. ***The expression "normal operation of the aircraft" implies something which is common and generic to air travel as we know it e.g. loss of pressure resulting from landing descents and ordinary seating arrangements according to the classes of travel, and not with particular exit characteristics of particular aircraft employing particular jetways at particular airports.***

Conclusion

49. This appeal must be allowed. Contrary to the District Judge's conclusion, I am satisfied that the Appellant sustained her ankle injury as a result of an accident within the meaning of Article 17 of the Convention.

Key Points:-

1. There is no need to prove negligence, it is a form of strict liability.

2. To establish breach the claimant had to establish (a) that there had been "an unexpected or unusual event" such as spilling of coffee on a passenger by a flight attendant, and (b) that it was "external", in the sense that it had not been caused or contributed to by the claimant, i.e the claimant had not contributed to the accident.

3. Case Law suggests that when the injury indisputably results from the passenger's own internal reaction to the usual, normal, and expected operation of the aircraft, it has not been caused by an accident, and Article 17 of the Warsaw Convention cannot apply. For example in DEEP VEIN THROMBOSIS & AIR TRAVEL GROUP LITIGATION (2005) a passenger who suffered deep vein thrombosis on a normal international flight would not have suffered an "accident" under the Warsaw Convention on International Carriage by Air 1929 Art.17 and could not succeed in a claim against the airline, because an accident for the purposes of Art.17 required an unexpected or unusual event or happening that was external to the passenger.

4. To succeed the accident must occur on broad the aircraft or in the course of embarking or disembarking.

5. PHILIP KING V BRISTOW HELICOPTERS LTD : RE M (A CHILD BY HER LITIGATION FRIEND CM) (2002) confirms that only physical injury will recover. Article 17 Warsaw Convention made provision for compensation for bodily injury sustained on board an aircraft. It did not provide for compensation for mental injury or illness that was not caused by or did not amount to injury to the body.

What about damages?

Article 21 sets out:-

Article 21 – Compensation in case of death or injury of passengers

1. For damages arising under paragraph 1 of Article 17 not exceeding 100,000 Special Drawing Rights for each passenger, the carrier shall not be able to exclude or limit its liability.

2. The carrier shall not be liable for damages arising under paragraph 1 of Article 17 to the extent that they exceed for each passenger 100,000 Special Drawing Rights if the carrier proves that:

(a) such damage was not due to the negligence or other wrongful act or omission of the carrier or its servants or agents; or

(b) such damage was solely due to the negligence or other wrongful act or omission of a third party.

Therefore damages will be assessed by the Law of England and Wales, in the normal way i.e by reference to the JC guidelines for general damages.

Limitation

Article 35 sets out:-

> *Article 35 – Limitation of actions*
>
> ***1. The right to damages shall be extinguished if an action is not brought within a period of two years, reckoned from the date of arrival at the destination, or from the date on which the aircraft ought to have arrived or from the date on which the carriage stopped.***
>
> *2. The method of calculating that period shall be determined by the law of the court seized of the case.*

It should be noted section 33 Limitation Act would not apply. There are also no special rules for children.

Costs – can be recovered in the normal way i.e. on the standard basis.

Article 22 – Limits of liability in relation to delay, baggage and cargo

> *6. **The limits prescribed in Article 21 and in this Article shall not prevent the court from awarding, in accordance with its own law, in addition, the whole or part of the court costs and of the other expenses of the litigation incurred by the plaintiff, including interest.** The foregoing provision shall not apply if the amount of the damages awarded, excluding court costs and other expenses of the litigation, does not exceed the sum which the carrier has offered in writing to the plaintiff within a period of six months from the date of the occurrence causing the damage, or before the commencement of the action, if that is later.*

Costs can be recovered but the airline can protect itself on costs by making an offer as above.

CHAPTER FOUR
HOLIDAY ILLNESS AND THE WOOD V TUI UK CASE

There are potentially three ways in which breach of duty could be found in relation to a holiday illness claim. Many people who will buy this book will have purchased the first holiday illness / food poisoning book. Since the publication of that book, and since the authors of the book were writing an updated book, it is necessary to provide a detailed analysis of the recent Court of Appeal case – *Wood v TUI UK Limited (Case number 3YJ60681),* and its effect on gastric illness claims. The defendants in Wood essentially sought to challenge the proposition that breach of duty under *section (4) (2) of the Supply of Goods and Services Act* 1982 in holiday illness claims is strict and furthermore argued that evidence of local standards is required in every case.

The source of contention in Woods was whether the 1982 act applies to food in the context of the Transfer of Goods. The Judge in *Antcliffe* said:- "*The contract involves an agreement to "transfer" those goods to the Claimants. It is perhaps not the sort of transfer to be found in a more commercial context, but the provision of food for consumption necessarily involves its transfer to the consumer. HH Judge Stephen Davies referred to this being the "supply of a product" at paragraph 60 of his Judgment in Kempson v First Choice".* The Defendants in Wood denied that food and drink served as part of a restaurant meal are 'goods' and asserted that they were not 'sold' or 'supplied' within the meaning of section 4 of the 1982 Act and Section 14 of the 1979 Act. Rather they argued that the arrangement of food and drink as part of a holiday contract was a 'service' within the meaning of section 13 and that the Defendant's duty, consistent with its duty under Regulation 15 of the 1992 Regulations and pursuant to *Hone v Going Places*, was to exercise only reasonable skill and care.

It is helpful before launching into an analysis of *Wood* to remind practitioners of the salient points in the cases supporting an interpretation of **strict liability**. *Kempson* and *Antcliffe* set out the following matters relevant to the application of the *Sales of Good Act 1979 and the Supply of Goods and Services Act 1982*:-

The main case is *Kempson v First Choice Holidays and Flights Limited 7 June 2007 Birmingham County Council.* Although only first Instance this case is authority for the principle that where a holiday package included the provision of meals by a foreign hotel, the tour operator through which the holiday had been booked was under a strict obligation to provide food which was of satisfactory quality and reasonably safe for reasonable consumption. That test was to be applied in substantially the same manner as the test defined by the *Sale of Goods Act 1979 s.14*. The relevant section of the Judgment is as follow:-

> "*As already noted, the Claimant's case is that:*
>
> *(1) The obligation to supply food of satisfactory quality is a strict obligation, rather than a fault-based one, as of course is the obligation imposed by section 14 of the Sales of Goods Act 1979.*
>
> *(2) The same principle applies to the obligation to supply food which is reasonably safe for the Claimant's reasonable consumption.*
>
> *(3) Even if it is necessary to show fault, it is clear to me that there was fault in undercooking the scrambled egg because undercooking a food which might be subject to salmonella infection its in itself a breach of duty to take reasonable care*'.

It went on:-

> "*63. In my judgment, the same argument applies not just to the obligation to supply food of satisfactory quality, but also to the obligation to supply food which is reasonably safe for human consumption. If food is supplied which is not reasonably safe for human consumption, so long as the food is consumed in way which is reasonable to consume it, then in my judgment the term is breached even through the supplier may not have been at fault*".

65. Furthermore, there would in my judgment appear to be nothing unfair in applying the obligation to the case of meals supplied by a foreign hotel as a part of a package, even if the informed consumer might be taken to know that the meals would not be supplied by the tour operator itself. This is because a) the tour operator would still have the statutory defence under Regulation 15 (2) and b) the tour operator would always have, or at least it would be open to the tour operator to stipulate for a contractual right of indemnity against the supplier of the meal".

67. I therefore conclude that the obligation is a question of a strict obligation, and that it is to be applied is substantially in the same manner as the test defined by section 14 of Sale of Goods 1979. In Particular, by sub section 142B, this expressly includes the safety of the goods in question. Subject to the further point raised by the Defendant I would have little hesitation in holding that the obligation was breached by the supply of undercooked scrambled eggs contaminated with salmonella in sufficient qualities to render an infective dose to the eater".

70. However, that is very different from holding that the law requires every claimant who is seeking to prove a breach of such obligation to adduce evidence as to local standards of safety, failing which he simply cannot succeed. In my judgment, a claimant in such as the present is not required to undertake such an exercise. If the defendant wishes to contend that local standards permit certain foods to be served in a particular country even though they would not have been reasonably safe for human consumption, that would be a matter for the defendant to plead and prove".

The other main case is *Antcliffe v Thomas Cook* 4 July 2012, Birmingham County Court. A family that had booked an all inclusive holiday with a tour operator was awarded damages for breach of contract after contracting food poisoning during the holiday. The hotel food was the source of infection and there was an implied term under the Supply of Goods and Services Act 1982 s.4(2) that the supply of goods, which included food, would be of a satisfactory quality. The

Claimants in the case argued that the 1982 Act imposed strict liability and said that "*once it is proved the claimants illnesses were caused by eating at the hotel, there is liability*". The Court said:-

> "*103. Satisfactory quality is an objective standard. The function of section (4) (2) is to establish a general standard of quality which goods are required to reach as opposed to the fitness of goods for some particular purpose*".
>
> "*105. The inescapable fact was that the food was contaminated with ETEC or salmonella which was capable of causing some quite serious illness. It is very hard to see how the reasonable man could begin to find that as being of satisfactory quality. I find that the food was not of satisfactory quality and that the Defendant is in breach of contract. The contract had not been properly performed. It follows then claimants can establish liability*".
>
> "*106. The same result would follow from the implication that of a term the food be reasonably fit for purpose under the same Act. Food is commonly supplied to be eaten. If it make you ill, can it be said to be reasonably fit for purpose? In my Judgment no it cannot*".

If liability is not strict, what is left?

The case of *Antcliffe* is helpful on this point and indeed *Antcliffe* was pursued in a number of ways as set out in the Judgment as follows:-

> "***Firstly he submits that because the contract between the parties provided for the supply of goods (food) and services, the 1982 Act applied and section 4(2) had effect to imply into it a term that those goods were to be of a satisfactory quality.*** *The allegation is that the Defendant was in breach of that term, for by its supplier (the hotel) it supplied contaminated food or drink to the Claimants, causing them to contract ETEC or salmonella.* ***Mr Young's submission is that the fact that the food was contaminated means that it was not of "satisfactory quality" for the purposes of section 4, and that it is not necessary to prove a failure to exercise reasonable care and skill by the hotel supplying***

> ***the food, whatever the applicable standard may be. He submits that once it is proved that the Claimants illnesses were caused by eating at the hotel, there is liability.*** *In the sense that no negligence is required, it is a form of strict liability.*
>
> ***Secondly that by the failure of its supplier to take reasonable care in the provision, preparation and supply of food or drink and/or the supplier's breach of local laws, the Defendant is guilty of the improper performance of the package holiday contract contrary to regulation 15 of the 1992 regulations.***
>
> ***Thirdly that the Defendant itself was in breach of an implied term of the sort found in Wilson v Best Travel and/or a duty of care to like effect,*** *as more fully pleaded out in paragraphs 5 and 6 of the Amended Particulars of Claim"*

Essentially, therefore, there is strict liability under SGSA 1982 (s4.2) (the subject of Wood), and that in providing food that is contaminated the service provided was not of reasonable skill and care; i.e. improper performance of the contract under Regulation 15 or section 13 Supply of Goods and Services Act 1982. A claim in negligence can also be pursued but any common law claims would have to be assessed by applying evidence of local standards as set out in *Wilson*.

What do the cases say about local standards in holiday illness cases?

In *Antcliffe* the Defendant argued :-

> *"The Defendant also denies that the hotel failed to exercise reasonable skill and care in the provision preparation and supply of food to the Claimants.* ***The positive case is that the standard to be applied is the local one, and that the evidence available suggests that whatever those standards were, they were met.***
>
> *Mr Candlin accepts that there is an implied term that food supplied to the Claimants as part of the package holiday was to be of satisfactory quality; see paragraph 53 of his Closing submissions. He*

relies in particular upon the provisions of section 4(2A) of the 1982 Act, by which:

.. goods are of satisfactory quality if they meet the standard that a reasonable person would regard as satisfactory, taking account of any description of the goods, the price (if relevant) and all other relevant circumstances

Mr Candlin submits that a consideration of what a reasonable person would regard as satisfactory requires (amongst other things) a consideration of whether the care taken to see that the food was safe was reasonable; see paragraph 55 of his Closing submissions. He also submitted that a reasonable person would understand that food provided in the Dominican Republic might cause stomach upsets and the like, and that despite all reasonable efforts a pathogen might not be eradicated. Those matters would inform the standard. He disputes Mr Young's submission that there is a form of strict liability once it is shown that the Claimants became ill as a result of eating contaminated food at the hotel.

At paragraphs 5 and 6 of his skeleton argument, he accepts that by operation of the 1992 Regulations the Defendant is liable for the acts and omissions of its hotelier and suppliers in resort which occasioned a breach of the holiday contract to the extent that such breach was caused by a failure to exercise reasonable skill and care. ***He accepts that local standards of food hygiene will apply to determine whether or not the hotel took reasonable care. He emphasises that this is the Dominican Republic. He also accepts that terms may be implied into the contract between the parties of the nature identified in <u>Wilson</u>. There are issues as to the detail of those terms"***

The Judge also said as to local standards:-

"I have already considered the factual issues relevant to this aspect, and much of the relevant issues of expert evidence. I ***<u>had written evidence as to the law in the Dominican Republic from Lludelis Espinal, an Attorney at Law in the Dominican Republic [261-</u>***

273]. The local regulations quoted give only general guidance; so for example Article 17 of Application Rule 2332 requires that food be "kept at an appropriate temperature". As to a claim, the Civil Code requires "fault" to bring a civil claim (for tort as we would know it). If a duty, its breach and consequent damage are proved then there is a claim; see paragraph 7 on [271]. As I read it, a Claimant needs to establish negligence.

That does not really assist in terms of local hygiene standards. The parties agree that it is the local standard which I must apply; ***see Evans v Kosmar Holidays Ltd** [2008] 1 WLR 297. Neither Mr Horrocks nor Dr Dinsdale can assist particularly. Mr Horrocks refers to the Codex Alimentarius Commission, which is an International Body set up in 1963 by the WHO and the UN. The Dominican Republic is a member. The Commission has produced Guidance standards, and HACCP principles have been applied; see paragraph 6.2 of his report [323]. HACCP is an approach.* ***Whilst there is no direct evidence from the hotel of how they approached the matter, the audit report demonstrates that a HACCP system was in place.*** *Not only that, its operation was reviewed regularly by external contractors.* ***There were areas for improvement, but overall the results were good. Standing back, that is not the sort of evidence which speaks of negligent failures to maintain the relevant standards of hygiene.***

The height of the Claimants case here is set out at paragraph 6.6 of Mr Horrocks report [324], where he says this:

In summary, whilst there may have been no direct legal obligation on the hotel complex to implement a strict HACCP system, in practice HACCP is no more than a system for ensuring that hygiene standards are consistently achieved and that foods prepared in establishments such as hotels are fit and safe for consumption. ***In this sense HACCP is a system for the self management of a food operation and therefore no more than a vehicle for achieving safe food. Regardless of any local legal provisions covering operational hygiene stands at this hotel complex,***

if the court concludes that the primary pathogens responsible for the guests illness were bacterial rather than viral, then I believe that any reasonable and responsible hygiene regime applied by the hotel, that incorporated the safe storage, preparation, cooking, handling and service of food would have avoided the guests being infected.

I also refer to his conclusions at paragraphs 8.1 and 8.3 [332-3].

Professor Pennington takes a simple approach to this matter, and says in effect that if these people were infected as he says they were, then the kitchen was negligent; see [314], ***This rather avoids the point, for it is the duty and standard of care in the Dominican Republic in 2005 that I have to consider.*** *This hotel did operate a HACCP system. That may be recognition of a requirement that it did so, or it may not be. I have found that the Antcliffes were infected by food from this hotel. That may demonstrate that there was a failure to comply with the relevant local standard, or it may not.*

Mr Young submits that the Defendant has failed to deny a breach of local standards, or to call any evidence about them; see paragraph 39 of his written closing submissions.

He refers to breaches of international standards. Mr Candlin submits that the Codex Alimentarius Commission's Code is advisory. Neither it nor the FTO agreement gives rise to a supra-national standard or the sort of "uniform international regulation" *envisaged by Phillips J in <u>Wilson v Best</u> @ 358c. The Codex suggests the adoption of HACCP principles, no more; see paragraph 8 of his skeleton argument. I also note in passing the approach to FTO standards at [25] in the judgment of Richards LJ in <u>Evans v Kosmar Villa Holidays Ltd</u>.*

<u>I am not satisfied that the evidence I have establishes what the relevant standard is.</u> *It is plainly not right to assume that the same standards apply as they would in England and Wales. Mr Candlin referred me to Mrs Antcliffe's description of the Dominican*

> *Republic as "third world".* ***Absent any further evidence on this point, I am not satisfied that the Claimants have proved that the hotel breached the relevant local laws or standards relating to food hygiene".***

In *Kempson* the Court said:-

> ***"The further point raised by the Defendant is that the question as to whether or not the food supplied was of satisfactory quality and/or reasonably safe for the Claimants' reasonable consumption can only be answered by reference to local standards of food safety and, since the Claimants had failed to adduce any evidence as to local standards, it could not establish breach of those obligations.***
>
> *This is a point which is argued by analogy with the position which applies where the court is considering whether or not a tour operator has discharged the duty of reasonable care imposed on him under s. 13 of the Supply of Goods of Services Act 1982: see Wilson v Best Travel Ltd [1993] 1 All ER 353 (QBD, Phillips J), Codd v Thomas (2000) (unreported) (Court of Appeal), and First Choice v Holden (2006) (unreported) (QBD, Goldring J).* ***In such cases, as is well known, the standard by which the service provider is to be judged is the standard applicable to the country in which the service is provided, as opposed to the standard applicable in this country.***
>
> *I can well see that any local standards relating to the safety or otherwise of food supplied by a foreign hotel under a package holiday may be 'relevant circumstances' which, by analogy with section 14(2A) of the Sale of Goods Act 1979 may be taken into account when assessing whether or not the goods are of satisfactory quality. However, that is very different from holding that the law requires every claimant who is seeking to prove a breach of such obligation to adduce evidence as to local standards of food safety, failing which he simply cannot succeed. In my judgment, a claimant in such as the present is not required to undertake such an exercise.* ***If the defendant wishes to contend that local standards permit certain***

foods to be served in a particular country even though they would not be regarded as reasonably safe for human consumption, than that would be a matter for the defendant to plead and prove.

Here, the Defendant has never attempted to plead or to prove any difference between English and Greek standards, and I have no doubt that this is because there is no difference between the two. *This is not a case, such as could possibly be conceived, where a hotel laid on a special banquet of local specialities, one of which inevitably involved some risk of food poisoning. I can well see that a tour operator might well in such a case be able to establish a defence based on local standards as a relevant circumstance, subject perhaps to the issue as to whether or not a sufficient warning was given"*

What about pursuing a negligence claim i.e. failure to take reasonable care under Regulation 15 in the proper performance of the holiday contract?

The case of *Hone v Going Places* confirmed the duty under Regulation 15 did not impose an absolute or strict liability on the other party to the contract, namely the tour operator or travel agent. It said as to the common law duty of care:-

"***Regulation 15(1) ensures that Going Places was responsible for the proper performance of the contract by those supplying the relevant service*** *- in this case the air carriage -whoever it was that actually performed that service".*

"*Of course, absolute obligations may be assumed. If the brochure or advertisement, on which the consumer relies, promises a swimming-pool, it will be a term of the contract that a swimming-pool will be provided. But, in the absence of express wording, there would not be an absolute obligation, for example, to ensure that the holiday-maker catches no infection while swimming in the swimming-pool.* ***The obligation assumed will be that reasonable skill and care will be taken to ensure that the pool is free from infection. A similar term will be implied in relation to transportation in the***

absence of any express wording, viz that reasonable skill and care will be exercised. A travel agent or tour operator does not usually, for example, promise that the pilot of the aeroplane will not have a heart attack."

"Regulation 15(2) provides for the other party to the contract to be liable for any damage caused to the consumer by failure to perform the contract or by the improper performance of the contract. The present case is not a case of failure to perform. It can only be a case of improper performance. It is only possible to determine whether it is a case of improper performance by reference to the terms of the contract which is being performed. To my mind, regulation 15(2) does not give the answer to the question, "What is improper performance?" Rather it is a requirement of the application of regulation 15(2) that there should be improper performance. That can only be determined by reference to the terms of the contract. <u>There may be absolute obligations, eg as to the existence of a swimming-pool or any other matter, but, in the absence of the assumption of an absolute obligation, the implication will be that reasonable skill and care will be used in the rendering of the relevant service. There will thus be no improper performance of the air carriage unless there is an absence of reasonable skill and care in the provision of that service</u>. <u>If, as here, it is the claimant who seeks to rely on regulation 15(2), then he has to show that there has been improper performance".</u>

In *Antcliffe* the Court said about the negligence claim:

"My view is that the evidence does not establish that there was a causative failure on the part of the Defendant to take reasonable care in selecting the hotel or monitoring its performance (or the like). The systems they had for carrying out internal checks at the hotel were not of the best, but in the absence of some knowledge on the part of the Defendant of failings in the kitchen, persistent complaints about the temperature of the food or regular outbreaks of food poisoning, it does not seem to me that there is the factual basis for successful claims in this area. *If the parties* *require a more detailed analysis of this aspect of the claim, I will provide further reasons"*

In Wood, the Court said the following about the negligence claim:-

> *"**I can see a basis for the allegation the Claimants make, but I have concluded***
>
> ***that there is not enough to prove negligence or the like. This is not a case where there is an identifiable candidate for the source of the infection, as there was in Kempson. There the finding was that the probable cause of the Claimant's illness was under-cooked scrambled egg, and that necessarily involved the conclusion that the relevant member of staff failed to cook the egg properly; see at paragraph [73] of FIH Judge Davies QC's judgment in that case.** But there is nothing like that here. Nor do I have any expert evidence from a microbiologist or a food safety expert to assist me. 1 am conscious that the Claimants' ability to investigate the matter at trial has been limited by the lack of an opportunity to cross-examine a relevant witness from the hotel. **But on the evidence I have it is at least as possible that the infections which Mr. and Mrs. Wood picked up at the hotel were a result of isolated events**"*

In Kempson the Court said as to the negligence claim and applying the test for local standards:-

> *"I should also go on to consider the question as to whether or not the Claimants had discharged the burden of proving fault, if - contrary to the conclusion I have already reached - they **need to do so. In my judgment, subject again to the 'local standards' point raised by the Defendant, they have done so.** That is because, as I have already found, the most probable cause of the salmonella infection was consumption of undercooked scrambled egg, and in my judgment that necessarily involves the conclusion that the relevant member of staff failed to scramble the egg so that it was thoroughly and properly cooked. That, in my judgment, is a clear act of negligence in producing food which was not reasonably safe for human*

consumption, for which the Hotel and thus the Defendant is vicariously liable.

Returning then to the question of local standards, I fully accept that as a matter of general principle the issue as to the standard of care to be expected from a supplier of services in a foreign country is to be determined according to the standards applicable in that country at the time of the incident in question, rather than by the standards applicable in this country, if different. I also accept that one cannot circumvent the need for proof of local standards where that is necessary by simply purporting to apply the general duty to take reasonable care to the facts of the case. I note that the Holden case was a case where the allegation against the hotel was in substance a breach of the general duty of care owed by an occupier of premises to a lawful visitor to those premises.

Returning then to the question of local standards, I fully accept that as a matter of general principle the issue as to the standard of care to be expected from a supplier of services in a foreign country is to be determined according to the standards applicable in that country at the time of the incident in question, rather than by the standards applicable in this country, if different. I also accept that one cannot circumvent the need for proof of local standards where that is necessary by simply purporting to apply the general duty to take reasonable care to the facts of the case. I note that the Holden case was a case where the allegation against the hotel was in substance a breach of the general duty of care owed by an occupier of premises to a lawful visitor to those premises.

I also accept that it is not a question of pleading foreign law, but a question of establishing the relevant local standard, which is not a matter of foreign law. *That said, it seems to me that if a defendant wishes to contend that it is not at fault because the local service supplier has adhered to applicable local standards, then that is something which normally ought to be pleaded in the Defence under CPR Part 16.5.*

However, I do agree with the Claimants' submission that this cannot be a statement of invariable application in every case. To take an example, what if this case had concerned the Claimants suffering injuries as a result of a collision caused by a coach driver, hired to take them on an excursion arranged as part of the package holiday, taking a corner too fast and driving off the road? On the Defendant's approach, it would have been necessary for the Claimants to adduce evidence from someone with professed expertise in road safety standards in Corfu to give evidence that it was not acceptable in Corfu for a driver to take a corner so fast that he drove off the road, even if the Defendant had neither pleaded that there was a different approach to road safety in Corfu or adduced evidence to that effect. With respect, that seems to be to be a nonsense. Whilst the Defendant could of course argue that this requirement could always be avoided if the Claimants had asked for and obtained a formal concession that there was no difference in standards, even that seems to me to be an unnecessary and irrelevant requirement. There would be no danger in such a case of the trial judge in the English court wrongly applying English standards to determine the nature of the obligation imposed on the foreign service supplier".

*"**<u>On the facts of this case, there is not and never has been any dispute as to the applicable standards here.</u>** In paragraph 5 of its Defence the Defendant admitted without qualification paragraph 5(4) of the Particulars of Claim, which pleads an objective standard. **The witness statements tendered by the Defendant did not contain any suggestion that local food standards in some way recognised and permitted a risk to be taken so far as the service of undercooked egg or poultry dishes was concerned. The experts both agreed that salmonella infection is avoidable if correct food standards are adopted.** The Hotel manager and head chef both agreed under cross-examination that it would be wholly unacceptable to provide contaminated food to its guests. These are wholly unsurprising statements, whether one is considering the position in this country or in Corfu. In my judgment it would be a denial of justice if I were to conclude that what I otherwise decided to be a*

proven case failed simply because the Claimants had failed to adduce evidence in relation to something which was not, and never had been, in dispute.

Furthermore, in my judgment there is an obvious and relevant difference between a case - such as the present - ***where the standard is not in dispute, and the question is whether or not the local service supplier achieved that standard, and cases - exemplified in the reported decisions to which my attention has been brought - where the question is whether or not taking a certain step is something which was reasonably required of the local service supplier under the applicable local standards****. So for example in the case of Wilson v Best Travel the question for consideration was whether or not the Greek hotel was obliged to fit safety glass to the patio door, as was required by English standards, but not by Greek standards. In the case of Codd v Thomsons the question was whether or not the Spanish hotel was required to provide alarm devices or emergency instructions in the lift when that was required under English regulations but not under Spanish regulations, and in Holden v First Choice the question was whether or not Tunisian standards required the hotel to put in place a regime such as that which the Recorder in his judgment under appeal found was required of them, namely 'a safety system and protocol in place which includes periodic inspections and responding to people walking around with bottles or glasses or whatever to check the stairs for not only liquid but broken glass or anything like that'.* ***If the issue in this case had been, for example, whether the Defendant was obliged to comply with the applicable English regulations in relation to the temperatures at which hot and cold food should be stored, in contrast to what were apparently the applicable Greek regulations, then I accept the position would have been different****. This is not however such a case.*

I do not read the judgments relied upon by the Defendant as support for the proposition that in every case where fault is alleged by a holidaymaker in relation to a foreign holiday it is necessary for the Claimant to adduce expert evidence as to local standards. On the facts of this case, I do not consider that it is necessary for the Claimants to do so in order for them to succeed in establishing fault.

I therefore conclude that insofar as the Claimants are required to prove fault, they have done so, and the Defendant's objection that they cannot succeed because they have failed to adduce evi-dence of local standards fails"

Wood v TUI UK Limited – The Outcome in the Court of Appeal

The case of Wood (at first instance) ultimately succeeded under section 4.2 and 13 of the SGSA 1982 because:-

"Having found that Mr. and Mrs. Wood contracted their illnesses from food or drink which they were given to the hotel, I come to the issues which arise in relation to the terms to be implied pursuant to the 1982 Act. There are two. ***The first, regardless of whether or not there is an implied term to this effect, is whether the food or drink supplied was of satisfactory quality.*** *A similar point was considered by His Honour Judge Stephen Davies Q.C. in the Kempson case. There the Defendant admitted that there was a term that the food supplied by the hotel would be of satisfactory quality and reasonably safe for the Claimant's reasonable consumption, although it is not clear what the source of that admitted obligation was. The issue is dealt with at paragraphs [58] to [72] of the judgment. Whilst I had no submissions which dealt directly with the issues considered by Judge Davies QC, it is right that 1 record that 1 have reread this section of his judgment, and note his passing reference to the 1982 Act and paragraph [64]. That imports an objective standard.* ***It is what a reasonable person would consider satisfactory, and what "reasonably satisfactory" means requires the court to take account of all the relevant circumstances - that being a reference to the provisions of section 4(2)(a) of the 1982 Act. Those circumstances would include the fact that reasonable care is taken to prepare the food, but no system is perfect and, as we began, this was the Dominican Republic.***

This line of argument arose in the Antcliffe case and is dealt with at paragraphs [102] to [106] of my judgment. I put to Mr. Jones in argument the conclusions I expressed in that case: that the focus of the requirements of the term was on the quality of the food or drink, and that I found it hard to see how' food, which was infected with some bacteria which made you this ill, could be considered to be of satisfactory quality. Again, he was characteristically succinct. He thought he could do no better than Mr. Candlin, who was Counsel for the Defendant in Ancliffe. I have considered the point afresh, but for the reasons I give in my judgment in Ancliffe ***I have concluded that the food or drink which caused these illnesses was not of satisfactory quality"***

"***The second issue is whether there is any term implied as to satisfactory quality.*** *The issue w-as not argued in Kempson, and in Ancliffe the Defendant conceded that section 4 of the 1982 Act applied and that the food supplied by the hotel was to be of satisfactory quality, even though it was part of a package holiday to the Dominican Republic.*

I find that this contract is a contract for the supply of goods for the purposes of the 1982 Act. The fact that services are also supplied does not prevent it from being so. *(See section 1(3)). I also find that it is a contract for the supply of services for the purposes of the same Act. The fact that goods are also provided does not prevent it from being so.* ***There is nothing odd in that result. Many contracts will involve the supply of goods and services. There may be one contract, one agreement between the parties, but that does not mean that that one contract cannot qualify both as a contract for the transfer of goods and as a contract for the provision of services under the terms of this Act. There is support for that construction in the words and structure of the Act.***

Secondly, there is nothing in the Act to say that a contract for the transfer of goods cannot be a contract for the supply of services (for the purposes of this Act) at the same time. Whereas there is a term which says that a contract can be a contract for the transfer

of goods, whether or not services are also provided (and vice versa). *If the Claimants' construction is adopted, the provisions of the Act are easy to apply.* ***For having qualified, either as a contract for the transfer of goods, or for the supply of services, or both, the relevant implied terms are triggered, not simply as to quality or taking reasonable care, but also as to title, sale by sample and the other implied terms set out in Parts 1 and/or 2. Those in Part 1 will be the terms referable to the transfer of goods, and those in Part 2 referable to the supply of services.***

To require the court to choose between the two regimes is unnecessary. They can sit together. Indeed, it seems to me that the reason for sections 1(3) and its counterpart, section 12(3), is to enable that outcome. If the court were required to choose which type of contract this was, to pigeon hole it as either as a Part 1 contract or a Part 2 contract, it would be undertaking a task which would fail to recognise that it was a contract for both the transfer of goods and the provision of services, and I can see no good policy reason for that.

Further, that task may be a difficult one. I say at once that identifying the predominant nature or purpose of the contract in this case is not difficult, for I would accept Mr. Jones' submission that the provision of food was a relatively minor part of the package. The flights and accommodation would be the major element, and they relate to the provision of services. But it is not difficult to think of cases where the question would be finely balanced.

This potentially difficult choice would determine the regime to be applied. So that if it were a contract for services, the goods transferred as part of that contract would not have to be of satisfactory quality. Either there would be no implied terms to their quality or there would be some resort to the implied terms to reasonable skill and care (or back to the common law). *If the goods were made or adapted by the seller, that might work, but how would such a term (that to take reasonable skill and care) apply, for example, if the goods were simply bought in by the supplier and sold on?*

> *There are cases where a Part 2 implied term can be made to fit the transfer of goods, but applying a term designed to apply to services seems an odd thing to legislate for. And. if the contract were predominantly a contract for the supply of goods, how does the term as to "satisfactory quality" apply to the services provided? It is hard to see how that can be made to fit. One example which came up in submissions was a contract for the sale of a carpet. Mr. Jones submitted that it would be a contract for the transfer of goods, even if the carpet seller agreed to fit it. In which case, what would be the position if the carpet was of wonderful quality but it was fitted badly? There would be no statutory implied term. It would be surprising if the Act had gaps in its provision in that way.*

Consequently the Court found:-

> ***Consequently, I find that there was an implied term in this contract that the food and drink consumed by the Claimants at this hotel should be of satisfactory quality pursuant to the 1982 Act. That term was breached, and the Defendant is liable on that basis."***

The Court, in essence, at first instance upheld breach of duty under section (4) (2) and s13 of the 1982 Act (both for the supply of goods and services). The Defendants argued on appeal to the Court of Appeal in *Wood* that there is no such implied term for the transfer of goods and that strict liability does not apply. The Court of Appeal Judgment in *Wood* handed down on 16 January 2017 making the following points:-

a) Judgment was upheld in favour of Mr. Wood and the Defendant and the Court finds that "*the contract between First Choice and Mr. and Mrs. Wood was a contract both for the supply of services and the supply of goods*".

b) It went on "*the goods were not of satisfactory quality because the food in question was contaminated*". The Court said that whether goods "*are of satisfactory quality is a question of fact but where food is con-*

taminated with bacteria that causes severe illness it is difficult to imagine that it could be described as satisfactory quality".

c) The Judge raised a number of other very important causation points which requires careful analysis:-

a) "*Mr Aldous spoke of First Choice being potentially liable for every stomach upset which occurred on one of their holidays and the term 'strict liability' was mentioned. That is not the finding of the judge or the conclusion that he applied the correct legal approach dictates....* ***The Judge was satisfied in the evidence that Mr and Mrs Wood suffered illness as a result of contamination of the food or drink they had consumed".*** It must follow, it is argued, that the Court is saying that the claimant must still prove (as in Antcliffe), that the cause of the infection was contaminated food or drink from the hotel, but arguably closes the door that evidence of local standards is required in every food poisoning case. The Judgment does not mention local standards at all.

b) The Court said "*such illness can be caused by any number of other factors. Poor hygiene is an example but equally bugs can be picked up in the sea or swimming pool. In a claim for damages of this sort, the claimant must prove that food or drink provided was the* ***cause*** *of their trouble and the food was not satisfactory*". It is argued that this will be evident via the medical evidence. The medical expert needs to be as specific as possible concerning medical causation and whether it was the food or drink that was the cause of the complaints. Medical reports that merely state that the illness was caused by '*poor hygiene at the hotel*' may be not good enough. They must refer to the cause being contaminated food or drink.

c) The Court then said "*it would not be enough to invite a Court to draw an adverse inference from the fact someone was sick....Contamination must be proved and it might be difficult to prove that food or drink was not of satisfactory quality in the absence of evidence of others who had consumed the food being similarly afflicted*". In other words lone cases of food poisoning may be difficult but if a family/ group is effected, that may point to evidence of causation of food poisoning.

d) The Court also said "*the evidence deployed in the trial window shows the hotel was applying standards of hygiene and monitoring of their food which were designed to minimize the chances the food was dangerous. The application of high standards in a given establishment, when capable of being demonstrated by evidence, would inevitably lead to some caution before attributing illness to contaminated food in the absence of clear evidence to the contrary*". In other words, where the Defendant has a reasonable system, the Court would have to be very sure there was good evidence of contamination before establishing the illness was caused by it. Claimants will likely to be very wary of cases where there is evidence of a reasonable system and poor evidence of contamination. In these cases, the claimant would need to point to something very specific as to the cause of the infection to succeed.

e) The Court found "*the judge heard evidence not only from Mr and Mrs Wood but also from suitable experts and in light of the medical position recorded in the records Mr Wood's admission to hospital in both the DR and the United kingdom. In my view he was correct to conclude that provision of contaminated food amounted to a breach of the implied condition found in section 4 (2) of the 1982 Act. In those circumstances it is unnecessary to consider Mr Weir's alternative argument based upon the common law. I would dismiss the appeal*". The Court of Appeal did not even determine C's alternative Appeal based upon common law negligence as it found the standard to be applied was the implied term under the SGSA 1982 s4.2.

f) In essence, the Court of Appeal appears to be saying if the Claimant can show evidence of contaminated food, breach of duty will be established under the SGSA 1982. It seems to follow the claimant will have to be more specific as to how the food was contaminated such as it was undercooked etc. and very generalized complaints i.e. animals around the swimming pool etc. will have little relevance if they do not relate specifically to the food. The points raised by the Court of Appeal appear to relate to medical causation issues and how the Court is to approach that issue.

g) Sir Brian Leveson issued a warning "*I agree that it will always be difficult (indeed very difficult) to prove that an illness is a consequence of food or drink that was not of a satisfactory quality, unless there is cogent evidence that others have been similarly effected and alternative explanations would have been excluded*". Therefore lone cases of food poisoning (in the absence of any credible evidence by the claimant they for example were served with a raw burger) and those with a system may prove to be very difficult to prove on the balance of probability.

h) The case of *Wood v TUI* is welcome guidance from the Court of Appeal on these issues and where for example a family / group / couple is all ill from the same hotel, the Court of Appeal appears to be suggesting these are strong cases and prima facie evidence there was contamination from the food and/or drink.

i) It is yet to be seen how far defendants will pursue their evidence-based defences. In the writers' opinions, even a strong defence based on a high standard of hygiene and procedures is risky if taken to trial and the cost of doing so for every such case would probably be prohibitive. How likely is it that a defendant will pay for its hotel manager, chef and external auditor to come to England to attend a trial over a low-value claim? There have been such cases but it may not be practical to do so in the numbers of cases now being brought and claimants who hold their nerve may well still succeed. There is real litigation risk to defendants in such cases as the case law cited above shows.

CHAPTER FIVE
PACKAGE CLAIMS UNDER THE 1992 REGULATIONS AND EVIDENCE OF LOCAL STANDARDS

All accidents claims involving slips and trips abroad, are likely to rely upon evidence of local standards in the jurisdiction, where the accident takes place. This Chapter will also look at the applicability of the 1992 Regulations to these claims. The Package Travel, Package Holidays and Package Tours Regulations 1992, SI 1992/3288 will sometimes apply, rendering the tour operator liable for the negligent acts and omissions of the supplier of goods and services under the holiday contract.

Similarly, claims are brought in contract and particularly under the *Supply of Goods and Services Act 1982* and/or under the *Consumer Rights Act 2015 (if a post 1 October 2015 booking)*, the Claimant could apply, as these claims are effectively for breach of the holiday contract brought under English Law, but applying evidence of local standards.

Most accident abroad claims for example, slips and trips in foreign hotels, and claims such as accidents in relation to hotel glass doors, injuries in lifts, defects with the pool etc will be brought under the Package Claims 1992 Regulations. If the claim is not a package within the meaning of the 1992 Regulations, it is unlikely the Claimant Solicitor would wish to proceed on a CFA, as it would mean suing in the hotel's local jurisdiction. There is a separate Chapter in this book, which looks at the law surrounding the applicability of the 1992 Regulations, and whether a claim is likely to fall within the Regulations or not.

Firstly there are a number of useful cases that examine the applicability of local standards evidence. In ***GARETH DAVID CODD (A CHILD, SUING BY HIS UNCLE & LITIGATION FRIEND, MR T GRIFFITHS) V THOMSON TOUR OPERATIONS LTD (2000),*** it was held that there was no requirement for a hotel abroad to comply with safety regulations made under English law. The relevant sections from the Judgment are as follows:-

> "*The claimant's claim arose out of an accident which occurred on 28th October 1996, when he caught the middle finger of his right hand in the door of a lift. The claimant was born on 17th January 1986 and was 10 years and when the accident occurred. He brought these proceedings by his uncle, Mr. Griffiths, who acts as his next friend and conducted the proceedings before the trial judge and has conducted this appeal before us.*
>
> *3. The defendants, Thomsons, are well known holiday tour operator. On 3rd September 1996 the claimant's father booked his holiday for himself and on behalf of his wife and the claimant's two sisters at the Hotel Corfu at Cala D'or in Majorca. They went on holiday on 19th October 1996 for a period of ten days. By the terms of the agreement made between them the defendant agreed that they would be liable for injuries caused by the negligence of its suppliers, in this case the Hotel Corfu.*
>
> *4. On the last day of the holiday, 28th October 1996, the claimant entered a lift in the hotel with his two sisters who were older than him. The lift was one of a fairly familiar type. There was an outer door which was hinged and an inner sliding door which close automatically when the outer door had been closed. The claimant and his sisters went in to the lift and neither of the doors shut.* ***It appears that the outer door had, for some reason, jammed before it reached its proper resting place in the door frame. Gareth put his right hand round the door and pulled it towards him. The door then shut quickly and caught his right middle finger as a result of which he sustained a serious injury to it.***
>
> ***5. Judge Roach was trying the issue as to liability only. The defendants accepted that they would be liable to pay damages to the claimant if negligence was established against those who were responsible for running and managing the hotel.***

9. The judge had before him documentation which showed that, in accordance with Spanish law, the lifts at the hotel were examined on a monthly basis by managers. Mr Griffiths has stressed very strongly, and in my judgment perfectly understandably, that apart from the records that the inspections had taken place there was no disclosure from the hotel as to what work, if any, was done on the lifts or as to their state of repair and maintenance immediately before and immediately after Gareth's accident.

12. On page 11 of if his judgment the judge said in relation to the documents:

What do I make of those records? I think I can make this of them, that they show, according to Spanish law, because that is the certificate that is upon them, that this lift and this installation was looked at with a frequency of once a month, and that this lift and this system survived that inspection, and was found to be working, by record, adequately and safely."

13. Then a little later on he said:
I am driven to the conclusion, on the balance of probability, that there was a maintenance system in operation and an inspection system in operation, in accordance with Spanish law, as the certificates indicate."

16. In addition to alleging that the accident occurred as a result of the failure to maintain the lift properly, it was alleged on behalf of the claimant that there was no emergency equipment or proper advice in the lift as to what to do if the door did not close, or if the lift failed to operate correctly. ***The judge said in his judgment that there were no regulations in Spain which required safety signs to be posted in lift or a requirement that there should be an emergency alarm or emergency procedure in the lift if the door did not close or the lift became stuck.***

17. There is such a requirement in English law under current regulations governing the installation and use of lifts and we

have those regulations with our documentation**. **The lift did not comply with those regulations but complied with Spanish legislation.** In those circumstances the judge concluded that it could not be said that the managers of the hotel were negligent in failing to install alarm devices or instructions as to what to do in an emergency. **The judge recorded that the lift performed as a standard unit to lifts throughout Spain. Accordingly he arrived at the conclusion that negligence had not been established against the hotel owners or managers and, in consequence, it was not established against the tour operator.

*22. Mr Griffiths then submits that the judge was in error in not applying the British standards to this particular lift in the hotel in Cala D'or with the result that there was a breach of duty according to English law. That is not a correct approach to a case such as this where an accident occurred in a foreign country. **The law of this country is applied to the case as to the establishing of negligence, but there is no requirement that a hotel for example, in Majorca is obliged to comply with British Safety Standards: see Wilson v Best Travel Limited [1999] 1 All ER at 353".***

In Wilson v Best Travel Ltd [1993] 1 All ER 353 the Court said:

*'**...there are bound to be differences in the safety standards applied in respect of the many hazards of modern life between one country and another...the duty of care of a tour operator is likely to extend to checking that local safety regulations are complied with**. Provided that they are, I do not consider that the tour operator owes a duty to boycott a hotel because of the absence of some safety feature which would be found in an English hotel unless the absence of such a feature might lead a reasonable holidaymaker to decline to take a holiday at the hotel in question...".*

There are a number of points that arise from this in relation to local standards:-

1. The burden will be upon the claimant to produce a CPR 35 compliant report as to local standards. This may cover statutory, regulatory or customary local standards.

2. English law in terms of causes of action, evidence and procedure will be applied but the court will apply local laws when deciding if there has been a breach of duty and expert evidence regarding local standards applying any such duty will need to be provided via an appropriate expert.

3. The report will likely be obtained with reference to local practice for example in a slipping case near a hotel pool, evidence of local standards in relation to non-slip flooring would be required. In a defective hotel room glass door case i.e no warning stickers on the glass, evidence would be required as to the local standard or practice from perhaps a building surveyor who constructs hotels.

4. Strict liability will not apply (unless at present in a food poisoning case and subject to *Wood v TUI*), the Claimant must prove negligence to the civil standard.

5. The Claimant could also argue that *res ipsa* applies i.e the facts speak for themselves, but again it would be a very risky argument without going to Trial without evidence of local standards. It is this element that makes these claims unsuitable for the small claims track, if the small claims track limit rises to £5,000, as the Court will almost always need evidence of local standards on such a case, and that report needs to be paid for.

The case of *FIRST CHOICE HOLIDAYS & FLIGHTS LTD V PATRICIA HOLDEN (2006),* is a good example of what happens where the claimant fails to produce evidence of local standards. A claim for personal injuries suffered when falling down some hotel steps in Tunisia failed because it had not been shown that the hotel had fallen below the standards of safety of a Tunisian hotel. The Court said that the local standard could not be inferred from what might well be a higher standard in a particular hotel. The Claimant had failed to show that the hotel had fallen below the standards of safety of a Tunisian hotel by failing to have a system such as that which the recorder held should have existed. The Court held it was for the Claimant to prove that the Defendant fell short of the standards applicable in Tunisia and no evidence in that regard had been adduced by the Claimant.

The case of *Lougheed v On the Beach Limited [2014] EWCA Civ 1538* dealt with a Claimant who sustained a fractured ankle and shoulder when she slipped on a patch of water on polished granite stairs. It again gave some warning, as to the failure to provide evidence of local standards. The key sections from the Judgment are as follows:-

> "*The party flew to Spain on 14 August 2009. On the morning of 16 August Mrs Lougheed slipped and fell while going down a flight of polished granite steps which had non-slip grooves cut into them. At the time Mrs Lougheed was holding on to the handrail on her side of the steps with her left hand.* ***The judge found, resolving disputed evidence, that she had slipped on a patch of water on the steps.***
>
> *Mrs Lougheed suffered a fracture dislocation of her right ankle, a fracture of the left shoulder and bruising to her lower back and bottom. It was agreed that if On The Beach was liable to her in respect of her loss, her damages in respect of her injuries and consequential financial loss should be quantified at £30,000. Mrs Lougheed contended that On The Beach was liable to her pursuant to paragraph 15(1) of the Regulations which provides:-*
>
> ***Liability of other party to the contract for proper performance of obligations under contract1.*** *The other party to the contract is liable to the consumer for the proper performance of the obligations under the contract, irrespective of whether such obligations are to be performed by that other party or by other suppliers of services but this shall not affect any remedy or right of action which that other party may have against those other suppliers of services."* ***Mrs Lougheed contended that the circumstance that water was deposited on the steps and/or allowed to remain there until she***

slipped upon it was indicative that the hotel had not exercised reasonable skill and care in the discharge of its obligations owed to her. That, she said, cast upon On The Beach an evidential burden to adduce evidence of the exercise of reasonable skill and care directed towards the avoidance of the steps becoming and/or remaining wet.

That case was concerned with safety regulations, as opposed to the standards adopted in routine maintenance and cleaning in order to ensure the safety of hotel guests. In principle however one would expect a common approach to both. ***Standards of maintenance and cleanliness vary as between countries and continents and indeed what is reasonably to be expected in a five star hotel in a Western European capital differs from what is reasonably to be expected in a safari lodge, however well-appointed. There may perhaps be certain irreducible standards in relation to life-threatening risks, but to expect uniformity of approach on a matter such as the frequency of inspection and cleaning of floor surfaces is unrealistic. An Englishman does not travel abroad in a cocoon.***

Holden v First Choice Holidays and Flights Ltd 22 May 2006, unreported, was a case decided by Goldring J, as he then was, under the Regulations. Mrs Holden fell down some stairs in a hotel in Tunisia. It was found that she had slipped on some spilt liquid, probably a spilt drink. The question arose as to the standards to be required of the hotelier and whether a member of staff was required to be stationed to monitor spillages on the staircase. The judge held that the duty of care was that set out by Phillips J in Wilson v Best Travel. He held that it was for the claimant to prove that the defendant fell short of the standards applicable in Tunisia. The claimant had adduced no evidence of such standards and there was no material before the court on the basis of which inferences could be drawn as to the content of those standards. The Recorder in the court below had drawn inferences as to the standards applicable from evidence concerning the care received by the claimant in hospital in Tunisia, and from evidence as to the standards applied by another company in another hotel. Goldring J rejected that approach.

At page 11D he said this:-

"It does not seem to me that one can infer a local standard from what may well be a higher standard in a particular hotel or by a particular company in particular circumstances. It is no substitute for evidence of what is local custom and what may be the local regulations."

In Evans v Kosmar Villa Holidays [2008] 1 WLR 297, a case decided under the Regulations, Richards LJ, with whom the other members of this court agreed, cited the passage above from the judgment of Phillips J in Wilson v Best and observed:-

"23. A claim such as that in Wilson v Best Travel Ltd would no doubt be put differently under the 1992 Regulations: since the tour operator is directly liable under those regulations for improper performance of the contract by the hotel even if the hotel is under independent ownership and management, ***the focus can be on the exercise of reasonable care in the operation of the hotel itself rather than in the selection of the hotel and the offer of accommodation at it. But I do not think that this affects the principle laid down as to the standard to be applied to a hotel abroad, namely that the hotel is required to comply with local safety regulations rather than with British safety standards. That was the approach in Codd v Thomson Tour Operators Limited (Court of Appeal judgment of 7 July 2000), in which the claimant had been injured while travelling in a lift at a hotel in which he was staying in Majorca.*** *The tour operator accepted that it would be liable (presumably under the 1992 Regulations) if negligence was established against those who were responsible for running and managing the hotel, but the judge found that liability was not established. The Court of Appeal dismissed the claimant's appeal, citing Wilson v Best Travel Ltd for the* ***proposition that there was no requirement for the hotel to comply with British safety stan-***

dards, and holding that there was no breach of local safety regulations and that there was no negligence by the hotel management either in relation to the maintenance of the lift or in relation to safety procedures."

In Evans the Court of Appeal decided that the hotel had no duty to guard the claimant, who was of full capacity, against the obvious risk of diving into the shallow end of a swimming pool. *There had in that case been no evidence to support the pleaded claim of non-compliance with local safety regulations, and that way of putting the case was not pursued at trial. As Richards LJ observed:-*

"24. In the present case, there was no evidence to support the pleaded claim of non-compliance with local safety regulations, and that way of putting the case was not pursued at trial. *In my view, however, it was still open to the claimant to pursue the claim on the other bases pleaded in the amended particulars of claim. What was said in Wilson v Best Travel Ltd did not purport to be an exhaustive statement of the duty of care, and it does not seem to me that compliance with local safety regulations is necessarily sufficient to fulfil that duty. That was evidently also the view taken in Codd, where the court found there to be compliance with local safety regulations but nevertheless went on to consider other possible breaches of the duty of care."*

Plainly compliance with locally promulgated safety regulations may not be the end of the enquiry. The regulations may be recognised locally as inadequate. There may be steps routinely taken to draw attention to risks tolerated by the local regulations, as for example the placing of a warning sticker on untoughened glass. One would not expect to find locally promulgated regulations governing the frequency with which a hotel floor should be either cleaned or inspected for the presence of spillages on which guests might slip. The standards by which the hotel is to be judged in its performance of such tasks as are unregulated, or where regulations are supplemented by local practice or are

recognised to be inadequate must necessarily, and on authority, be informed by local standards of care as applied by establishments of similar size and type.

Gouldbourn v Balkan Holidays & Flights Limited *[2010] EWCA Civ 372 concerned a claim under the Regulations by a novice skier who fell on a ski slope whilst on a skiing package holiday in Bulgaria which included six days instruction specifically designed for beginners at a local ski school. The main issue at trial was whether the ski instructor had exercised reasonable care and skill in his assessment, instruction and supervision of Mrs Gouldbourn.* ***The trial judge concluded that the instructor's conduct had to be judged against the relevant local standards****. There was no evidence as to the content of such local standards and the claim was accordingly dismissed. Referring to Holden, Leveson LJ, with whom Jacob LJ and Briggs J agreed, said:*

"18. This case has been taken to entrench the need for evidence of local standards and indeed in this case paragraph 1(d) of the Defence asserts that the ***relevant standard of care had to be judged by Bulgarian standards****, and this contention was not challenged either in reply or the skeleton submissions filed on behalf of Mrs Gouldbourn at the trial. Neither is a breach of the FIS [Federation Internationale de Ski] rules pleaded. In any event, argues Mr Poole, the FIS rules are general principles rather than regulations adopted by all skiing nations as best practice. They establish the general duty of care, that is to say in this case the duty never to allow a pupil to take risks beyond their capabilities, but the implementation of that duty, namely how a particular country goes about ensuring it, is a question of local standards and arrangements and, given that (sic) the absence of any evidence on this topic notwithstanding the clear identification of the issue in the Defence, the claim is rightly dismissed.19. It is a mistake to seek to construe the judgment of Phillips J as if it was a statute: see the observations of Richards LJ in Evans v Kosmar Villa Holidays PLC[2008] 1 WLR 297 at para 224 page 3068 to the effect that the case did not purport to be an exhaustive statement of the duty of care. Nevertheless it does identify*

a very important signpost to the correct approach to cases of this nature, which will inevitably impact on the way in which organisations from different countries provide services to UK tourists. To require such organisations to adopt a different standard of care for different tourists is quite impracticable. ***What might be required for American tourists may well be different to that required by a French or Western European tourist, itself different to that required by a Japanese tourist. Neither do I consider that the Regulations impose a duty on English tour operators to require a standard of care to be judged by UK criteria or necessarily western European criteria."***

Finally, Japp v Virgin Holidays Ltd *[2013] EWCA Civ 1371* ***was concerned with local building regulations.*** *Richards LJ, with whom Lewison LJ and I agreed, observed at paragraph 5 that:-*

"The courts have been consistent in following the approach in Wilson v Best Travel Ltd as to the applicability of local standards, though the legal framework has been altered to some extent by the Package Travel, Package Holidays and Package Tours Regulations 1992, regulation 15 of which provides that "[t]he other party to the contract is liable to the consumer for the proper performance of the obligations under the contract, irrespective of whether such obligations are to be performed by that other party or by other suppliers of services". *As was* ***observed in Evans v Kosmar Villa Holidays Ltd*** *[2008] 1 WLR 297,* ***para 23, since the tour operator is directly liable under the regulations for improper performance of the contract by the hotel even if the hotel is under independent ownership and management, the focus can be on the exercise of reasonable care in the operation of the hotel itself rather than in the selection of the hotel and the offer of accommodation at it. Thus, the particulars of claim in the present case pleaded an implied term, among others, that "the hotel, including the glass doors, would be of a reasonable standard and reasonably safe and would comply with all applicable local safety standards and regulations"; and the defence***

> ***effectively admitted that implied term, subject to the addition of the words "that were in force" at the end."***

The Court concluded in Lougheed, after considering all the authorities:-

> *"The judge recognised that standards may not be the same in Spain as in the UK and that there will be cases where the court is unable to draw an inference of want of care without sufficient evidence of Spanish standards. In my judgment this is just such a case, both because of the lack of relevant evidence on a point on which the Claimant bore the evidential burden, and because it was not a proper case in which to draw an inference, without more, of a lack of proper care. I deal separately with the second point under Ground 2 below.* ***I would not however wish it to be thought that evidence of relevant local practice or standards can only be given by an expert witness called as such, or at any rate in the form of a report of an expert for the introduction of which evidence the permission of the court has been given. I agree with Miss Prager that it is ordinarily preferable that evidence of these matters should be given in that way, not least because both the opponent party and the court has the protection and the reassurance of the standard form of declaration given by any person who seeks to give expert evidence. A Claimant who chooses not to adduce such evidence in a case of this sort does so at his peril.*** *That is not however to say that the evidence could not in an appropriate case be given by an appropriately experienced and qualified individual who nonetheless did not put himself forward as professing expertise in the field.* ***Because cases are infinitely various, and the exigencies of litigation unpredictable, I would not wish to be over-prescriptive. However for the reasons I have given the point does not here arise because the evidence of Mr Lazaro did not in my view bear the weight which the judge put upon it".***

In terms of breach of duty, the case of *Hone v Going places Leisure Travel limited (2001 EWCA CIV 947),* confirms that there is no strict liability on the tour operator under regulation *15 of the Package Travel*

Regulations, but it did confirm that the Claimant had to prove on the balance of probabilities the Claimant *"failed to carry out its obligations with reasonable skill and care"*. This was confirmed in the High Court Authority of *Holden v First Choice (2006)* at paragraph D. The same case also confirmed the principle that the Defendant was *"liable for the Claimant for the proper performance of its obligations under the holiday contract by Reason of Regulation 15 of Package, Travel, Package Holidays and Package Tour Regulations 1992"*.

Regulation 15 of the 1992 Regulations says:-

> ***Liability of other party to the contract for proper performance of obligations under contract***
>
> *15.—(1) The other party to the contract is liable to the consumer for the proper performance of the obligations under the contract, irrespective of whether such obligations are to be performed by that other party or by other suppliers of services but this shall not affect any remedy or right of action which that other party may have against those other suppliers of services.*
>
> *(2) The other party to the contract is liable to the consumer for any damage caused to him by the failure to perform the contract or the improper performance of the contract unless the failure or the improper performance is due neither to any fault of that other party nor to that of another supplier of services, because—*
>
> *(a) the failures which occur in the performance of the contract are attributable to the consumer;*
>
> *(b) such failures are attributable to a third party unconnected with the provision of the services contracted for, and are unforeseeable or unavoidable; or*
>
> *(c) such failures are due to—*

(i) unusual and unforeseeable circumstances beyond the control of the party by whom this exception is pleaded, the consequences of which could not have been avoided even if all due care had been exercised; or

(ii) an event which the other party to the contract or the supplier of services, even with all due care, could not foresee or forestall.

(3) In the case of damage arising from the non-performance or improper performance of the services involved in the package, the contract may provide for compensation to be limited in accordance with the international conventions which govern such services.

(4) In the case of damage other than personal injury resulting from the non-performance or improper performance of the services involved in the package, the contract may include a term limiting the amount of compensation which will be paid to the consumer, provided that the limitation is not unreasonable.

(5) Without prejudice to paragraph (3) and paragraph (4) above, liability under paragraphs (1) and (2) above cannot be excluded by any contractual term.

(6) The terms set out in paragraphs (7) and (8) below are implied in every contract.

(7) In the circumstances described in paragraph (2)(b) and (c) of this regulation, the other party to the contract will give prompt assistance to a consumer in difficulty.

(8) If the consumer complains about a defect in the performance of the contract, the other party to the contract, or his local representative, if there is one, will make prompt efforts to find appropriate solutions.

(9) The contract must clearly and explicitly oblige the consumer to communicate at the earliest opportunity, in writing or any other

appropriate form, to the supplier of the services concerned and to the other party to the contract any failure which he perceives at the place where the services concerned are supplied.

The **Wilson case** defined the duty as:-

"*What is the duty of a tour operator in a situation such as this? Must he refrain from sending holidaymakers to any hotel whose characteristics, in so far as safety is concerned, fail to satisfy the standards which apply in this country? I do not believe that his obligations in respect of the safety of his clients can extend this far. Save where uniform international regulations apply, there are bound to be differences in the safety standards applied in respect of the many hazards of modern life between one country and another. All civilised countries attempt to cater for these hazards by imposing mandatory regulations. The* ***duty of care of a tour operator is likely to extend to checking that local safety regulations are complied with. Provided that they are, I do not consider that the tour operator owes a duty to boycott a hotel because of the absence of some safety feature which would be found in an English hotel unless the absence of such a feature might lead a reasonable holidaymaker to decline to take a holiday at the hotel in question.*** *On the facts of this case I do not consider that the degree of danger posed by the absence of safety glass in the doors of the Vanninarchis Beach Hotel called for any action on the part of the defendants pursuant to their duty to exercise reasonable care to ensure the safety of their clients*".

In terms of the duty in contract law, the Wilson case said this about English contract law:-

"*Duty of care*

Section 13 of the Supply of Goods and Services Act 1982 provides:

In a contract for the supply of a service where the supplier is acting in the course of a business, there is an implied term that the supplier will carry out the service with reasonable care and skill,

The nature of the services provided by a travel agent when arranging a holiday can vary enormously, depending on the nature of the holiday. ***I am satisfied, having read their brochure, that the service provided by the defendants included the inspection of the properties offered in their brochure****. Such service is implicit from a number of passages in their brochure, including, under the heading Important Information:-*

Brochure descriptions

Every effort has been made to ensure the accuracy of descriptions and information contained in this brochure. However, we are not always able to exercise day-to-day control over all the component parts of the holiday arrangements and it is always possible that an advertised amenity may be withdrawn or changed due to various reasons, for the purpose of energy or water conservation, lack of demand or for maintenance, renovation etc. We will advise you if we become aware of a major change but we cannot accept liability for the loss of an advertised amenity in such circumstances. Similarly we cannot accept liability for loss, damage or inconvenience unless caused by negligence on the part of our own employees. We would add that we do keep an eye on the accommodation.

In my judgment, ***one of the characteristics of accommodation that the defendants owed a duty to consider when inspecting properties included in their brochure was safety. The defendants owe their customers, including the plaintiff, a duty to exercise reasonable care to exclude from the accommodation offered any hotel whose characteristics were such that guests could not spend a holiday there in reasonable safety. I believe that this case is about the standard to be applied in assessing reasonable safety.*** *It*

> *is necessary at this stage to turn to the evidence in relation to the glass fitted in the doors of the Vanninarchis Beach Hotel".*

If the holiday contract post dates 1 October 2015, therefore the Consumer Rights Act 2015 may apply. There will therefore be sections of the Consumer Rights Act 2015, that will be relevant to contracts for holidays that were formed on or after 1 October 2015 as follows:-

> ***"49 Service to be performed with reasonable care and skill***
>
> ***(1) Every contract to supply a service is to be treated as including a term that the trader must perform the service with reasonable care and skill.***
>
> *(2) See section 54 for a consumer's rights if the trader is in breach of a term that this section requires to be treated as included in a contract"*

Key Points:-

1. For pre 1 October 2015 contracts The 1982 Supply of Goods and Services Act may apply.

2. For post 1 October 2015 contracts the relevant sections from the Consumer Rights Act 2015 will need to be included in the letter of claim and pleaded. The pleadings are complex and Counsel may be best engaged to draft the Particulars of Claim.

3. In almost every case, a local standards CPR Part 35 complaint report will be required, as to the local standard in the jurisdiction where the accident takes place. This should be obtained pre-proceedings to draft the Particulars of Claim. The recent case of *Chelton v Acromas Holidays* failed because even through the Claimants had called legal expert evidence on Portuguse Law they failed to address the test of reasonable skill and care under the holiday contract which would require evidence as to the maintenance systems inside that jurisdiction. Experts on local standards

should not really be lawyers but a specialist in the relevant field. For example, if it is defective flooring, a local engineer who can give evidence on that issue.

CHAPTER SIX
CAUSATION INVESTIGATIONS – MEDICAL CAUSATION ISSUES, GATHERING MEDICAL RECORDS AND CREDIBILITY ISSUES

Causation is one of the most important aspects when considering any accident abroad claim. The reason, of course, for this is that even if the Claimant can succeed on the issue of breach of duty the Claimant still has to prove causation in relation to the injuries sustained. This becomes even more important when the credibility of the Claimant is at issue between the parties, and before expensive investigations into breach of duty are undertaken, including local standards reports, which can be costly. This Chapter focus more upon physical injury claims as opposed to food poisoning claims, dealt with in the related book.

The Claimant of course will have to prove legal and medical causation on the balance of probability. Establishing causation at an early stage in the case will be as important as establishing breach of duty given that if the Claimant's case fails on the issues of causation, there is little point in establishing breach of duty in the first instance.

This Chapter will therefore concentrate solely on investigating causation in relation to Accident Abroad cases and focus on the early investigations to be undertaken in relation to such cases at the outset.

Early Investigation

Early investigation of causation is always going to be key in relation to an Accident Abroad case. This will be particularly important if the Defendant puts the Claimant on notice that causation is going to be an issue.

This inevitably leads to the question as to how causation can be investigated in relation to such a case at an early stage and how can it be investigated economically.

The issue of causation can be investigated economically in the following ways:-

Medical Causation

a) The Claimant's Solicitor will wish to obtain the Claimant's General Practitioner records and hospital records at the first opportunity. The Claimant's solicitor should carefully go through the Claimant's contemporaneous GP and hospital records as this will often provide clues as to the mechanism of the accident.

b) The Claimant's Solicitor will also likely wish to obtain a copy of the accident report form, and any witness evidence to check the mechanism of the accident is consistent with how the Claimant says it occurred.

c) If there is any variation in the notes, careful instructions will need to be taken from the Claimant as to the reason for any inconsistencies.

One has to bear in mind that sometimes the treating medical practitioner is in a rush at the Accident & Emergency Department or the hospital doctor may get it wrong in the heat of the moment but the Claimant's Lawyer should be particularly cautious if the mechanism of the accident claimed for has been described incorrectly to both the GP and the treating doctor in the Accident & Emergency Department. If there are any inconsistencies in contemporaneous medical records, the Claimant's solicitor can sometimes seek to interview the treating GP or hospital doctor in order to confirm if there is any explanation for the notes being incorrect.

If you are dealing with a tripping or slipping claim in a hotel, consider the mechanism of the claimant's fall if there are inconsistencies between the GP and the hospital notes. For example, if the claimant states that they tripped over on their right foot in the accident report form but the medical records suggest that the claimant had tripped up on their left foot and these are recorded contemporaneously post-accident this should give rise to caution. It is of course the case that sometimes there are credible explanations for inconsistencies but, in the writer's experience, the Courts tend to treat contemporaneous medical records as having high degree of credibility given that they are recorded shortly after the accident and often before it is known that a claim is being made arising out of a claim. This is also true of accident report forms, if they were checked and signed by the Claimant.

It may be argued that it is often very difficult for a Claimant Lawyer to get over serious inconsistencies as to the recording of the mechanism of the accident, without any supporting evidence in respect of the same.

Some commentators have argued that fraud in this area is on the increase given the tightening of the insurer's investigations into whiplash type fraud, and Claimant Lawyers need to be very careful it may be argued to ensure that the Claimant's evidence is credible in relation to the mechanism of the accident.

Recording The Accident Circumstances – The Contemporaneous Version of Events

It is extremely important that the Claimant's Solicitor obtains from the outset an extremely detailed version of events from the Claimant to the mechanism of the accident, and exactly how the injury was sustained, that can be tested later to test the credibility of the first version of events given by the Claimant.

It is important that the Letter of Claim gives enough information to the Defendant to investigate the claim at the outset.

Causation – The Common Themes

When one is investigating an Accident Abroad case (especially slipping and tripping claim in foreign hotels), common themes often arise in terms of the issue of causation and whether the breach of duty contributed to the injuries sustained. Some of these may be broadly defined as follows:-

a) In a slip/trip claim at a hotel – was the Claimant running or walking at the time of the accident? It is common sense that lots of accidents are caused through people running rather than walking. At the outset of the claim, detailed questions should be taken from the Claimant as to whether they were running or walking when the accident took place, for example was the claimant running near the pool when he or she slipped? If the Claimant was running when the accident took place careful consideration should be given to possible findings of contributory negligence.

b) Had the Claimant consumed alcohol and if so, how much and when? This question will be particularly relevant if the Claimant had consumed a lot of alcohol in close proximity to the accident time or if this is present in the GP/Hospital records, and may be particularly relevant for claims that occur on holiday. It may be argued that Claimant Lawyers should be particularly wary of Claimants who have consumed a large amount of alcohol prior to an accident, as this may sound in contributory negligence, if not to extinguish any finding of liability on behalf of the Defendant entirely if the Claimant was severely intoxicated at the time of the accident.

c) Did the Claimant trip or slip on holiday? In terms of the credibility of tripping claims, one needs to ask the Claimant carefully, at the outset of the claim, how the tripping incident occurred. For example, did the Claimant trip with the left or the right foot, did the foot go entirely into the hole and what caused the

Claimant to trip, did the Claimant's foot get caught on the edge of the defect, and in which direction did the Claimant fall?

d) Does the Claimant's version of events make sense in terms of the mechanism of the tripping claim? For example, if the Claimant's foot gets caught on the edge of a defect, they are likely to fall forwards and not sideways. Whereas, if the Claimant puts their foot in an open manhole, they are likely to fall to the side, given their entire body weight will have been taken away from them and they will fall towards the side by which the foot has fallen into the manhole. When looking at the Claimant's version of events, ask yourself does it make sense?

e) Was this a slipping incident? If someone slips, generally one would expect the claimant's evidence to be that their foot had gone from underneath them, and a witness will usually describe a lack of grip under foot or similar prior to the fall and they may describe "their feet going from underneath them".

f) It is always important to establish which foot the Claimant slipped on. Was it the Claimant's left foot or their right foot and again is their version of events credible with regards to the way that they fell and the way that they landed following the fall?

Summary

Therefore, when assessing claims at the outset, it is important that the Claimant's lawyer looks at all the potential contributory factors to an accident when looking at the issue of causation as well as basic credibility.

Given the recently increased allegations by insurers of fundamental dishonesty, it is essential that detailed instructions are taken from the Claimant at the outset of the claim as to the mechanism of the accident and the way in which it was caused and if there are any inconsistencies or any concerns the claimant's general practitioner and hospital records, together with the accident report form and witnesses evidence are obtained at the first opportunity in order to check the consistency of events.

Post-Jackson the Claimant's Lawyer may well be wary of progressing claims where there are such serious inconsistencies.

The Claimant's Solicitor must also ensure that the version provided to the GP or Orthopedic Surgeon is detailed and that the Claimant's Lawyer should check the consistency of the version given to the Claimant's medical expert, as compared to the version that was given to the Claimant's Lawyer at the outset of the case and any inconsistencies in this are addressed urgently at the outset of the case.

It may be argued that there is little room now to run cases where there are serious inconsistencies as to legal or medical causation between the version of events in the Letter of Claim, the GP records, the Accident and Emergency notes, and the version that is given to the Claimant's medical expert.

If there are serious inconsistencies in the versions of events provided which lack explanation, the Claimant's lawyer may at this stage, give serious consideration as to whether it is a claim that should be litigated.

CHAPTER SEVEN
QUANTUM – QOCS / COSTS IN RELATION TO ACCIDENTS ABROAD; DISCLOSURE; AND PRE-ACTION PROTOCOLS

Quantum – Special Damages

Loss of Enjoyment Claims and Diminution in Value

This is one of the most common claims in an accidents abroad case and will usually be the largest head of special damages. In *Jarvis v Swan Tours* the Court said the award was "*for the disappointment, the distress and upset and frustration caused by the breach*". A special holiday such as a wedding or honeymoon or a holiday with a specific purpose is always going to attract higher damages, than, for example, a beach holiday with no planned activities. Awards generally range between £500 at the lower end up to £5,000 for a failed wedding. The reader should always refer to *Kemp* for specific examples.

Alongside a claim for loss of enjoyment will usually be a claim for the diminution in value of the holiday, that is, a claim for the cost of the actual holiday that could not be enjoyed due to the accident. This may well be a *pro rata* percentage reduction based upon then period of actual illness but not necessarily. The timing of the illness could mean that an important planned activity could not be undertaken that was the main purpose of the holiday. An example of that could be an illness preventing the holiday-maker from seeing the Northern Lights in Lapland on the one day they were visible during his hospital stay. Both heads of loss and the methods of calculation were considered in detail in the case of *Antcliffe v Thomas Cook*:-

> "*Diminution in Value and Loss of Enjoyment*

The claim for diminution in the value of the holiday is not simply a mathematical calculation based on the cost of each day of the holiday; see Ward LJ in Milner at paragraph [46]. There is no complete loss of bargain. *The first week of the holiday passed enjoyably enough although the disruption to the second week afflicted the whole of the family to some extent. Mr Young asks me to have in mind the fact that the children were separated from their parents, and that they were not looked after as promised on the return trip home. He submits that awards of £500 each for the 15‘ and 5"‘ Claimants and £250 each for the other Claimants are appropriate here, and that a further award for loss of enjoyment should be made in at least the same sum. At paragraph 27 of his skeleton argument and again at paragraph 60 of his closing submis-sions Mr Candlin submits that I should award two thirds of the value of the holiday under this head, taking care not to allow for the illness Mr Antcliffe, Tara and Rory suffered from, because no claim is made for that.*

In a note dated 2 July 2012 Mr Young asked me to review the decision I made on this point in the draft Judgment. He was right to do so. Unfortunately Mr Young was not at the handing down of this Judgement and Mr Candlin had not been provided with a copy of Mr Young's note. I heard oral argument from Mr Candlin, and from Mr Crow who appeared for the Claimants. ***Mr Candlin accepts that in some cases there may be an award for diminution and a further sum for loss of enjoyment. He submits that this is not such a case. Having read paragraphs 29 and 32 of Ward LJ's Judgment in Milner I am against him on that. His second submission is the stronger one, namely that there is overlap between the two awards, and the potential for a timber overlap with awards which include a sum for loss of amenity. The sums involved are not great but there should be an award which reflects the loss of enjoyment to all in this family as well as the diminution in the value of their holiday.*** *The parties are content if that is a global award. I will increase the award from the figure in the draft of £2,103 (that being Mr Candlin's figure) to £3,000.*

That is to be divided in a ratio of 2/7ths to Mrs Antcliffe and Tiah and 1/7"' to the other Claimants"

In (1) **TERENCE MILNER (2) CYNTHIA MARY MILNER v CARNIVAL PLC (T/A CUNARD) (2010)**, the Court looked at the correct measure of award to be made in a claim for a ruined holiday. The Court said:-

"The issue

1. The issue, said to be of importance for the travel industry, is this: what is the correct measure of damages for a ruined holiday?

The appeal

2. On 14th May 2009 His Honour Judge Shaun Spencer Q.C. sitting in the Bradford County Court, awarded the claimants, Mr and Mrs Terence Milner, £22,000 made up as to £2,500 each for the diminution in the value of their cruise on the luxury liner, Queen Victoria, and £7,500 each for their distress and disappointment when the cruise did not match their expectations, so £10,000 each. He also awarded Mrs Cynthia Milner £2,000 for her wasted expenditure on her wardrobe of formal dining gowns. The defendant, Carnival Plc, which trades as Cunard, appeals with permission granted by Sir Simon Tuckey who said "This case may provide the opportunity to give authoritative guidance on the appropriate measure of damages in "holiday" cases."

The facts

3. It is necessary to set out the facts in some detail. On 19th June 2006, almost eighteen months in advance of her sailing, Mr and Mrs Milner booked their passages on the maiden world cruise of the Queen Victoria. This cruise was to depart from Southampton on 6th January 2008 for New York, thence to Los Angeles via the Panama Canal, on to Honolulu, bound for Australasia, Hong

Kong, around south-east Asia, India, through the Suez Canal and the Mediterranean, returning to Southampton 106 days later.

4. The cost of their passage was £65,558, discounted by 10% to £59,052.20. This may seem a lot of money and a very expensive holiday but, as the appellant points out, the price breaks down to £557 per day, £3,900 per week, to cover travel, accommodation, food and entertainment of the highest standard for fifteen weeks.

The measure of damages

27. It is trite law that the measure of damages is such compensation as will place the claimants, so far as money can do so, in the same position as they would have been in had the contract been properly performed. The task is to compare and contrast what was promised and what was received, acknowledging that money cannot truly compensate for this deficit. As Lord Morris of Borth-y-Gest observed in Parry v Cleaver [1970] A.C. 1, 22

"But a money award is all that is possible. It is the best that can be done."

Doing the best one can is hardly the most enlightening guidance for those who have to perform the task, but I am not sure I can improve upon it.

28. It is always useful to bear in mind the observations of Lord Hoffmann in Banque Bruxelles Lambert SA v Eagle Star Insurance Co Ltd [1997] A.C. 191, 211A:

"Before one can consider the principle on which one should calculate the damages to which a plaintiff is entitled to compensation for loss, it is necessary to decide for what kind of loss he is entitled to compensation."

29. In a case like this the following aspects command attention. Firstly, compensation for pecuniary loss – the diminution in

value: the loss here is the monetary difference between what was bought and what was supplied. The task is to assess the amount by which the advertised holiday turned out to be less in money terms than the customer had paid for it.

30. Secondly, compensation for consequential pecuniary loss: this would cover out of pocket expenses such as the cost of alternative accommodation, the cost of alternative travel arrangements and so forth.

31. Thirdly, compensation for physical inconvenience and discomfort: it has long been established that damages for personal inconvenience "where it is sufficiently serious" *is recoverable: see Hobbs v London and South Western Railway Company (1875) L.R. 10 Q.B. 111, 117 per Sir Alexander Cockburn C.J. There Mellor J. said at p. 122:*

"... for the mere inconvenience, such as annoyance and loss of temper, or vexation, or for being disappointed in a particular thing which you have set your mind upon, without real physical inconvenience resulting, you cannot recover damages. That is purely sentimental and not a case where the word inconvenience as I here use it would apply."

This principle was applied in Stedman v Swan's Tours (1951) 95 Sol Jo 727 where instead of enjoying superior rooms with a sea view in a first class hotel, the holiday party found that the rooms reserved for them were very inferior and had no sea view.

They were unable to obtain accommodation elsewhere, and in the result the whole holiday was completely spoilt. Singleton L.J. said that:

"Damages could be recovered for appreciable inconvenience and discomfort caused by a breach of contract. It might be difficult to assess the amount to be awarded, but it was no more difficult than to

assess the amount to be given for pain and suffering in a case of personal injury."

In Farley v Skinner [2001] UKHL 49 [2002] 2 AC 732, the plaintiff was entitled to damages assessed at £10,000 for the significant interference with the enjoyment of his property cause by noise from aircraft flying over his land.

32. Fourthly, compensation for mental distress: the early view espoused by Mellor J. in Hobbs no longer holds sway. ***In Jarvis v Swans Tours Ltd [1973] 1 Q.B. 233 the court thought that those limitations were "out of date". That was a case of a skiing holiday which cost £64.45 but which "was pretty well ruined". Lord Denning held at p. 237/238:***

"***In a proper case damages for mental distress can be recovered in contract, just as damages for shock can be recovered in tort. One such case is a contract for a holiday or any other contract to provide entertainment and enjoyment. If the contracting party breaks his contract, damages can be given for the disappointment, the distress, the upset and frustration caused by the breach. I know that it is difficult to assess in terms of money, but it is no more difficult than the assessment which the courts have to make every day in personal injury cases for loss of amenity. Take the present case. Mr Jarvis has only a fortnight's holiday in the year. He books it far ahead and looks forward to it all that time. He ought to be compensated for the loss of it. …***

Here Mr Jarvis's fortnight's winter holiday has been a grave disappointment. It is true that he was conveyed to Switzerland and had meals and bed in the hotel. But that is not what he went for. He went to enjoy himself with all the facilities which the defendant said he would have. He is entitled to damages for the lack of those facilities and for his loss of enjoyment."

Edmund Davies L.J. said at p. 239:

"The court is entitled, and indeed bound, to contrast the overall quality of the holiday so enticingly promised with that which the defendant in fact provided. …

When a man has paid for and properly expects an invigorating and amusing holiday and, through no fault of his, returns home dejected because his expectations have been largely unfulfilled in my judgment it would be quite wrong to say his disappointment must find no reflection in the damages to be awarded."

That was a holiday which cost £63.45. The Court of Appeal increased his damages from £31.72 (one half of the cost of the holiday) to £125.

33. The next important case for present purposes is Jackson v Horizon Holidays Ltd [1975] 1 W.L.R. 1468. This was a four week holiday costing £1200. The accommodation and services provided were by any standard pretty ghastly. The County Court judge awarded £1100 without saying how he arrived at that figure. It was upheld by the Court of Appeal. The case established that the claimant could recover not only for his own inconvenience and stress but for those members of the family who were taking the holiday with him. Here Lord Denning said at p. 1472:

"In Jarvis ... it was held by this Court that damages for the loss of a holiday may include not only the difference in value between what was promised and what was obtained but also damages for mental distress, inconvenience, upset, disappointment and frustration caused by the loss of the holiday."

At p. 1473, he said:

"People look forward to a holiday. They expect the promises to be fulfilled. When it fails, they are greatly disappointed and upset. It is difficult to assess in terms of money; but it is the task

of the judges to do the best they can. I see no reason to interfere with the total award of £1100."

34. We were also referred to Adcock v Blue Sky Holidays Ltd, an unreported decision of the Court of Appeal dated 13th May 1980. There the cost of the holiday for five people was £98 per person. The county court judge allowed damages separately for the five holiday makers, having regard to how the breaches of contract affected each of them. He felt inhibited by Jarvis and Jackson and "would have approached the damages on a higher scale than [was] revealed by [those cases] "as appropriate". The Court of Appeal disagreed: as Bridge L.J. put it:

"I wholly fail to understand how the learned judge was able to extract anything from either of those case which prevented him from awarding the higher scale of damages which he said he was minded to award."

As Cumming-Bruce L.J. said:

"Contracts for holidays vary on their facts very greatly. The facilities offered by the tour company vary enormously from case to case. It would be a grave mistake to look at the facts in, for example, the Jackson case or the Jarvis case and compare those facts with the facts in another case as a means of establishing the measure of damages."

35. Those words of wisdom falling from Cumming-Bruce L.J. are salutary. I praise the industry of counsel and those instructing them in producing up to fifty-six "comparable" cases, practically every one of them reported only in the Current Law Journal and being no more than a précis of the proceedings in the county ***court. One of the few judgments of the High Court is Kepple-Palmer v Exus Travel [2003] EWHC 3529 (QB). Gage J. (as he then was) held:***

"44. In my opinion the claimant is entitled to a sum representing diminution in value of the holiday. In assessing this sum

I take into account that this was on any view a very expensive holiday. As such, the claimant and her party were entitled to expect very high standards. As I have found, what she was provided with fell well below these high standards. Doing the best I can, and taking into account what was provided, the location and the time of year, I assess damages under this head in the sum of £22,000 as will be obvious, I calculate this on the basis of a deduction of some 25% from the contract price.

45. In my opinion she is entitled to a sum representing loss of enjoyment. In this respect, I take into account that this was designed to be a very luxurious holiday, coming after her, and her family's, difficult year. This is, however, not the case of a family unused to holidays. To be able to afford the cost of such a holiday indicates a degree of financial resources from which I infer that that the claimant and her family are used to some of the more expensive things in life, including regular holidays. For that reason, in my judgment, the sum for the loss of the enjoyment must be modest; I assess it in the sum of £3,000."

I am not sure that the loss of enjoyment must necessarily always be more modest for the wealthy than the poor: the level of distress is surely measured by the extent of the failure to meet reasonable expectations and a luxury holiday of a lifetime for the rich can be as spoilt for him as the more modest holiday of a lifetime for the poor, unless of course the poor man will never be able to afford another whilst the rich man can ameliorate his disappointment by immediately booking another jaunt to make up for his loss. It is a question of fact and degree in each case.

Assessing the quantum of damages for inconvenience and distress

One place to look is to trace the awards given in holiday cases. As I have already pointed out at [35] above, this is not a particularly fruitful exercise because the facts of one case will be infinitely different from the facts of the next. For what it is worth, counsel's diligent analyses tend on the whole to show rather low awards. ***<u>One</u>***

of the highest for a ruined honeymoon was only £4,406, adjusted for inflation. The award in Jarvis is worth £1885 today and in Jackson £4101 for the family of five and in Keppel-Palmer £3499 for the party of six adults. Factors which will have a bearing on the amount of damages awarded in individual cases include the type of holiday so that a special occasion, such as a honeymoon, is likely to attract more damages than for an ordinary annual package holiday. Mr Christopher Lundie, for the appellant, gathered the known holiday cases in categories which show that the highest awards (£4406 to £4360) were to couples whose plans to marry abroad were wrecked; the disappointed honeymooners received from £321 to £1890; for other special holidays the range was £264 to £1161 and the run of the mill ruined holiday attracted between £83 and £1876. The nature of the breach will matter: the sports fanatic denied his sporting facilities will suffer more disappointment than his wife who is perfectly happy on a sunbed by the side of a pool. Thus the features of the holiday which were regarded as the primary features will make a difference.

In approaching the task of assessing damages, I accept that it is permissible to make the assessment under two heads, first the diminution in value and then the distress and disappointment. I do, however, stress that judges should always be alert to ensure that there is no duplication of damages and so it is always salutary to stand back and look at the sum of the two elements in the round before arriving at the figure to award.

43. As for the diminution in value of this holiday, the essence of the task, hypothetical though it may be, is to try to assess the difference between what the supplier contracted to provide and what was actually provided. It is essentially an assessment of a pecuniary loss. It is essential to exclude from this consideration how the client felt about the diminution in the service supplied, for therein lies the risk of a duplication of damages".

Therefore in summary, one always has to look in a holiday claim at a claim for diminution and a separate award for loss of enjoyment. However, one has to bear in mind, as with the *Carnival* Judgment that there may be some overlap between the two and the Court may well stand back and look at the picture overall. If the holiday is a special holiday such as a honeymoon or wedding, the damages for loss of enjoyment will be much higher and the Milner case provides some very useful guidance in this regard.

Key Points

1. The degree of loss of enjoyment and inconvenience will always be fact sensitive. 2 people on the same holiday may have different levels of disappointment.

2. Disappointment is not necessarily linked to the value of the holiday as a poor person may have more loss of enjoyment for losing his only holiday that year than a rich person who takes several holidays a year and who can easily book another one.

3. The damages can exceed the cost of the holiday but recent cases show relatively modest awards and there is likely to be overlap between diminution and loss of enjoyment.

QOCS and Costs

One of the key tactics when preparing an accidents abroad claim case is to have a high cogency of evidence and consistency (based upon the claimant's instructions) between the letter of claim, medical records, medical report and witness statement, and also explaining any inconsistencies in the witness statement. The Defendant will seek to challenge any inconsistencies between those documents and undermine the credibility of the case. If the Claimant has been found to have lied or exaggerated a claim, there are two ways in which this can have an implication in respect of the claim as follows:-

<u>The QOCS rules set out under 44.14:-</u>

QOCS will apply to these cases, provided there is a post LASPO funding arrangement as follows:-

48.2(1)

A pre-commencement funding arrangement is-

i. a funding arrangement as defined by rule 43.2(1)(k)(i) where……"
CPR 43.2(1)(k)(i) defines a funding arrangement as "an arrangement where a person has entered into a conditional fee agreement or a collective conditional fee agreement which provides for a success fee….."

Effect of qualified one-way costs shifting

44.14

(1) Subject to rules 44.15 and 44.16, ***orders for costs made against a claimant may be enforced without the permission of the court but only to the extent that the aggregate amount in money terms of such orders does not exceed the aggregate amount in money terms of any orders for damages and interest made in favour of the claimant.***

(2) ***Orders for costs made against a claimant may only be enforced after the proceedings have been concluded and the costs have been assessed or agreed.***

(3) ***An order for costs which is enforced only to the extent permitted by paragraph (1) shall not be treated as an unsatisfied or outstanding judgment for the purposes of any court record.***

Exceptions to qualified one-way costs shifting where permission not required

44.15 Orders for costs made against the claimant may be enforced to the full extent of such orders without the permission of the court where the proceedings have been struck out on the grounds that –

(a) the claimant has disclosed no reasonable grounds for bringing the proceedings;

(b) the proceedings are an abuse of the court's process; or

(c) the conduct of –

(i) the claimant; or

(ii) a person acting on the claimant's behalf and with the claimant's knowledge of such conduct, is likely to obstruct the just disposal of the proceedings.

Exceptions to qualified one-way costs shifting where permission required

44.16

(1) Orders for costs made against the claimant may be enforced to the full extent of such orders with the permission of the court where the claim is found on the balance of probabilities to be fundamentally dishonest.

In other words, if the Claimant proceeds to Trial and recovers zero, provided that the claim is not found to be fundamentally dishonest or one of the other exemptions above applies, the Court can still make a costs order but the Defendant will not be able to enforce it. A County Court Judgment would not be recorded against the Claimant in such circumstances.

The Defendant will only, in summary be able to enforce any order up to the amount of damages recovered by the Claimant.

QOCS protection may also be lost if the claimant fails to beat a defendant's Part 36 offer, but the defendant will only be able to recover costs up to the level of the claimant's damages.

QOCS of course arguably took away some of the need for After the Event insurance cover in relation to low value personal injury cases as, in effect, the Claimant's risk of paying the Defendant's costs has now been taken away except in very limited circumstances, such the failure to beat a Part 36 offer, but many Claimant Solicitors continue to advise clients to insure against this risk. There is also the matter of disbursements such as court fees and any experts' fees which the claimant will be potentially liable for if their claim does not succeed and they must be advised of such costs when considering ATE insurance.

Claimant Lawyers have to be wary of the rules surrounding fundamental dishonesty. In the case of *Gosling v Screwfix and Anr* (unreported, 29 March 2014) at Cambridge County Court, HHJ Moloney QC ordered the claimant to pay the defendant's costs of the action on an indemnity basis.

Section 57 Fundamental Dishonesty

57 – Personal injury claims: cases of fundamental dishonesty

(1) This section applies where, in proceedings on a claim for damages in respect of personal injury ("the primary claim")—

(a) the court finds that the claimant is entitled to damages in respect of the claim, but

(b) on an application by the defendant for the dismissal of the claim under this section, the court is satisfied on the balance of probabilities that the claimant has been fundamentally dishonest in relation to the primary claim or a related claim.

(2) The court must dismiss the primary claim, unless it is satisfied that the claimant would suffer substantial injustice if the claim were dismissed.

(3) The duty under subsection (2) includes the dismissal of any element of the primary claim in respect of which the claimant has not been dishonest.

(4) The court's order dismissing the claim must record the amount of damages that the court would have awarded to the claimant in respect of the primary claim but for the dismissal of the claim.

(5) When assessing costs in the proceedings, a court which dismisses a claim under this section must deduct the amount recorded in accordance with subsection (4) from the amount which it would otherwise order the claimant to pay in respect of costs incurred by the defendant.

(6) If a claim is dismissed under this section, subsection (7) applies to—

(a) any subsequent criminal proceedings against the claimant in respect of the fundamental dishonesty mentioned in subsection (1)(b), and

(b) any subsequent proceedings for contempt of court against the claimant in respect of that dishonesty.

(7) If the court in those proceedings finds the claimant guilty of an offence or of contempt of court, it must have regard to the dismissal of the primary claim under this section when sentencing the claimant or otherwise disposing of the proceedings.

(8) In this section—

- *"claim" includes a counter-claim and, accordingly, "claimant" includes a counter-claimant and "defendant" includes a defendant to a counter-claim;*

- ***"personal injury" includes any disease and any other impairment of a person's physical or mental condition;***

- *"related claim" means a claim for damages in respect of personal injury which is made— (a)in connection with the same incident or series of incidents in connection with which the primary claim is made, and (b)by a person other than the person who made the primary claim.*

(9) This section does not apply to proceedings started by the issue of a claim form before the day on which this section comes into force.

Therefore if the Court finds under section 57, the Claimant has exaggerated any part of the claim that goes to the heart of the Claim then it may lead to the entire claim being struck out – even the genuine parts. It is therefore very important that the claimant's schedule of loss is kept only to what is likely to be recoverable.

Pre-Action Disclosure, the Pre-Action Protocol and Types of Disclosure Pre Proceedings

The Pre-Action Protocol for personal injury claims applies as follows to accident abroad claims (under the 1992 Package Regulations):-

Letter of Claim

5.1 Subject to paragraph 5.3 the claimant should send to the proposed defendant two copies of the Letter of Claim. One copy of the letter is for the defendant, the second for passing on to the insurers, as soon as possible, and, in any event, within 7 days of the day upon which the defendant received it.

5.2 The Letter of Claim should include the information described on the template at Annexe B1. The level of detail will need to be varied to suit the particular circumstances. In all cases there should be sufficient information for the defendant to assess liability and to enable the defendant to estimate the likely size and heads of the claim without necessarily addressing quantum in detail.

5.3 The letter should contain a clear summary of the facts on which the claim is based together with an indication of the nature of any injuries suffered, and the way in which these impact on the claimant's day to day functioning and prognosis. Any financial loss incurred by the claimant should be outlined with an indication of the heads of damage to be claimed and the amount of that loss, unless this is impracticable.

5.4 Details of the claimant's National Insurance number and date of birth should be supplied to the defendant's insurer once the defendant has responded to the Letter of Claim and confirmed the identity of the insurer. This information should not be supplied in the Letter of Claim.

5.5 Where a claim no longer continues under either low value protocol, the CNF completed by the claimant under those protocols can be used as the Letter of Claim under this Protocol unless the defendant has notified the claimant that there is inadequate information in the CNF.

5.6 Once the claimant has sent the Letter of Claim no further investigation on liability should normally be carried out within the Protocol period until a response is received from the defendant indicating whether liability is disputed.

Status of Letters of Claim and Response

5.7 Letters of Claim and Response are not intended to have the same formal status as a statement of case in proceedings. It would not be consistent with the spirit of the Protocol for a party to 'take a point' on this in the proceedings, provided that there was no obvious intention by the party who changed their position to mislead the other party.

6. The Response

6.1 Attached at Annexe B2 is a template for the suggested contents of the Letter of Response: the level of detail will need to be varied to suit the particular circumstances.

6.2 The defendant must reply within 21 calendar days of the date of posting of the letter identifying the insurer (if any). If the insurer is aware of any significant omissions from the letter of claim they should identify them specifically. Similarly, if they are aware that another defendant has also been identified whom they believe would not be a correct defendant in any proceedings, they should notify the claimant without delay, with reasons, and in any event by the end of the Response period. Where there has been no reply by the defendant or insurer within 21 days, the claimant will be entitled to issue proceedings. Compliance with this paragraph will be taken into account on the question of any assessment of the defendant's costs.

6.3 The defendant (insurer) will have a maximum of three months from the date of acknowledgment of the Letter of Claim (or of the CNF where the claim commenced in a portal) to investigate. No later than the end of that period, The defendant (insurer) should reply by no later than the end of that period, stating if liability is admitted by admitting that the accident occurred, that the accident was caused by the defendant's breach of duty, and the claimant suffered loss and there is no defence under the Limitation Act 1980.

6.4 Where the accident occurred outside England and Wales and/or where the defendant is outside the jurisdiction, the time periods of 21 days and three months should normally be extended up to 42 days and six months.

6.5 If a defendant denies liability and/or causation, their version of events should be supplied. The defendant should also enclose with the response, documents in their possession which are material to the issues between the parties, and which would be likely to be ordered to be disclosed by the court, either on an application for pre-action disclosure, or on disclosure during proceedings. No charge will be made for providing copy documents under the Protocol.

6.6 An admission made by any party under this Protocol may well be binding on that party in the litigation. Further information about admissions made under this Protocol is to be found in Civil Procedure Rules ("CPR") rule 14.1A.

6.7 Following receipt of the Letter of Response, if the claimant is aware that there may be a delay of six months or more before the claimant decides if, when and how to proceed, the claimant should keep the defendant generally informed.

Disclosure Pre-Action

The Pre Action Protocol sets out as follows in relation to pre action disclosure:-

7. Disclosure

7.1 Documents

7.1.1 The aim of early disclosure of documents by the defendant is not to encourage 'fishing expeditions' by the claimant, but to promote an early exchange of relevant information to help in clarifying or resolving issues in dispute. The claimant's solicitor can assist by identifying in the Letter of Claim or in a subsequent letter the particular categories of documents which they consider are relevant and why, with a brief explanation of their purported relevance if necessary.

7.1.2 Attached at Annex C are specimen, but non-exhaustive, lists of documents likely to be material in different types of claim.

7.1.3 Pre-action disclosure will generally be limited to the documents required to be enclosed with the Letter of Claim and the Response. In cases where liability is admitted in full, disclosure will be limited to the documents relevant to quantum, the parties can agree that further disclosure may be given. If either or both of the parties consider that further disclosure should be given but there is disagreement about some aspect of that process, they may be able to make an application to the court for pre-action disclosure under Part 31 of the CPR. Parties should assist each other and avoid the necessity for such an application.

7.1.4 The protocol should also contain a requirement that the defendant is under a duty to preserve the disclosure documents and other evidence (CCTV for example). If the documents are destroyed, this could be an abuse of the court process.

In an accident abroad case (for example a tripping case in a foreign hotel under the 1992 Package Travel Regulations), the disclosure sought may be as follows:-

1) A copy of The Contract entered into between our client and your company;

2) Any documents relation to proof of purchase, including but not limited to booking form invoice and confirmation of booking;

3) Relevant brochure or marketing materials for the booking period, relating to the Package purchased by our client;

4) Health and Safety report for «NAME_OF_HOTEL_AddressName», including records of inspections and safety checks prior to our client's stay;

5) Housekeeping records for «NAME_OF_HOTEL_Organisation» for the period of 12 months prior to our client's stay;

6) Housekeeping records for «NAME_OF_HOTEL_Organisation» during and for the period of 12 months after our client's stay;

7) Records of any consumer complaints relating to tripping/ slipping claims at the «NAME_OF_HOTEL_Organisation» in «DESTINATION_COUNTRY_as_text» for the period of 12 months prior to our client's stay;

8) Accident/Illness report form relating to our client including details of any investigations carried out;

9) Onsite medical report forms;

It may be argued that a Pre-action disclosure application is more likely to succeed in encouraging holiday companies to settle claims. The disclosure of such information by a holiday company is likely to be unwanted, especially if there are multiple claims arising from the same premises. Therefore a PAD application may well be a quicker route to settlement than Part 7 proceedings. A costs warning should always be given before the PAD is issued, especially given the ordinary rule that the party providing the disclosure get the costs of the application in the absence of unreasonable conduct i.e. a refusal of the defendant to provide the disclosure.

Key Points

1. Always wait 1 day after your given deadline before issuing any PAD application. This avoids a submission by the Defendant on premature issue if they sent the disclosure on the last day for disclosing it but it did not arrive until the day after.

2. Be aware that CPR r.44.14 allows the Defendant to recover its costs of an interlocutory application (such as a PAD application) from the Claimant's damages even where QOCS applies up to

the value of damages recovered by the Claimant. Be particularly careful and precise in making such applications, therefore, in order to avoid a deduction from the client's damages.

CHAPTER EIGHT
ROME II – MOTOR ACCIDENTS ABROAD AND ACCIDENTS IN THE UK INVOLVING FOREIGN DRIVERS

This Chapter aims to look at both accidents in the UK and accidents that occur in other European Countries under Rome II.

Claims Against Foreign Insurers in the UK

In terms of an accident in the UK with a foreign driver sometimes an insurer will argue that there is no cause of action pursuant to the *2002 Regulations* as the vehicle is not normally based in the UK.

The *2002 European Communities Rights Against Insurers Regulations* set out:-

> *Interpretation*
>
> *2.—(1) In these Regulations—*
>
> *"the 1981 Order" means the Road Traffic (Northern Ireland) Order 1981(1);*
>
> *"the 1988 Act" means the Road Traffic Act 1988(2);*
>
> ***"accident" means an accident on a road or other public place in the United Kingdom caused by, or arising out of, the use of any insured vehicle;***
>
> ***"entitled party" means any person who is—***
>
> ***(a) a resident of a Member State; or***

(b) a resident of any other State which is a Contracting Party to the Agreement on the European Economic Area signed at Oporto on 2nd May 1992(3) and the Protocol adjusting the Agreement signed at Brussels on 17th March 1993;

"insured person" means a person insured under a policy of insurance satisfying the conditions set out in paragraph (3) of this regulation;

"vehicle" means any motor vehicle intended for travel on land and propelled by mechanical power, but not running on rails, and any trailer whether or not coupled, ***which is normally based (within the meaning of paragraph (2) of this regulation) in the United Kingdom.***

(2) The territory in which a vehicle is normally based is—

(a) the territory of the State of which the vehicle bears a registration plate; or

(b) in cases where no registration is required for the type of vehicle, but the vehicle bears an insurance plate or a distinguishing sign analogous to a registration plate, the territory of the State in which the insurance plate or the sign is issued; or

(c) in cases where neither registration plate nor insurance plate nor distinguishing sign is required for the type of vehicle, the territory of the State in which the keeper of the vehicle is permanently resident.

(3) For the purposes of these Regulations, a vehicle is insured if there is in force in relation to the use of that vehicle on a road or other public place in the United Kingdom by the insured person a policy of insurance (including a covering note) which fulfils the requirements of section 145 of the 1988 Act(4) or article 92 of the 1981 Order(5).

Rome II *(Rome II (European Regulations) Regulation EC No 864/2007)* and the various other Regulations which confirm a right of action against the MIB and/or the insurer. The 864/2007 Regulations shall apply from 11 January 2009, except for Article 29, which shall apply from 11 July 2008.

Article 4 says:-

> *"Article 4*
>
> *General rule*
>
> *1. Unless otherwise provided for in this* ***Regulation, the law applicable to a non-contractual obligation arising out of a tort/delict shall be the law of the country*** *in which the damage occurs irrespective of the country in which the event giving rise to the damage occurred and irrespective of the country or countries in which the indirect consequences of that event occur.*
>
> *2. However, where the person claimed to be liable and the person sustaining damage both have their habitual residence in the same country at the time when the damage occurs, the law of that country shall apply."*

Rome II will likely apply where the accident occurred England and Wales, and the Claimant can therefore sue within the jurisdiction. The Regulations continue in respect of liability of an insurer under the Regulations:-

> *"Article 18*
>
> *Direct action against the insurer of the person liable*
>
> ***The person having suffered damage may bring his or her claim directly against the insurer of the person liable to provide compensation if the law applicable to the non-contractual***

obligation or the law applicable to the insurance contract so provides".

The Law as to Rome II and application in England and Wales, was helpfully summarised in the case of **Jacobs v MIB,** where the Court helpfully set out in detail the history of Rome II and the various subsequent EC directives that apply in England and Wales, which have been summarised below:-

"EU legislation

Since 1949 motor insurers in a number of countries have operated what is known as the 'Green Card' scheme, under which the representatives of an insurer in one state handle claims on behalf of an insurer established in another state. The MIB was, and remains, the representative responsible for operating the 'Green Card' system in the United Kingdom. This system provided part of the foundation for legislation put in place by the European Union to ensure that compensation was available for those injured in road accidents regardless of the Member State in which the victim resided or in which the accident occurred.

(a) The First Motor Insurance Directive

The first step was taken in April 1972 *with the issue of Directive 72/166/EEC, known as the* ***'First Motor Insurance Directive'****, the material parts of which for present purposes provided as follows:*

"Article 3

1. Each Member State shall, subject to Article 4, take all appropriate measures to ensure that civil liability in respect of the use of vehicles normally based in its territory is covered by insurance. The extent of the liability covered and the terms and conditions of the cover shall be determined on the basis of these measures.

2. Each Member State shall take all appropriate measures to ensure that the contract of insurance also covers:

-- according to the law in force in other Member States, any loss or injury which is caused in the territory of those States; . . ."

I shall refer to this as "the First Directive".

(b) The Second Motor Insurance Directive

On 30th December 1983 the Council of Ministers issued Directive 84/5/EEC, known as the 'Second Motor Insurance Directive', which, among other things, provided for the establishment of guarantee bodies to provide compensation in cases where the vehicle responsible for the injury was uninsured or unidentified. *The material parts of the Directive (in the form in which it existed at the date of the accident) provided as follows:*

"Article 1

1. The insurance referred to in Article 3 (1) of [the First Motor Insurance Directive] shall cover compulsorily both damage to property and personal injuries.

. . .

4. Each Member State shall set up or authorize a body with the task of providing compensation, at least up to the limits of the insurance obligation for damage to property or personal injuries caused by an unidentified vehicle or a vehicle for which the insurance obligation provided for in paragraph 1 has not been satisfied.

The first subparagraph shall be without prejudice to the right of the Member States to regard compensation by that body as subsidiary or non-subsidiary and the right to make provision for the settlement of claims between that body and the person or persons responsible for the accident and other insurers or social security bodies required to compensate the victim in respect of the same accident. . . .

5. The victim may in any event apply directly to the body which, on the basis of information provided at its request by the victim, shall be obliged to give him a reasoned reply regarding the payment of any compensation.

. . .

7. Each Member State shall apply its laws, regulations and administrative provisions to the payment of compensation by this body, without prejudice to any other practice which is more favourable to the victim."

I shall refer to this as "the Second Directive".

(c) The Fourth Motor Insurance Directive

A third Directive was issued in 1990, but its provisions are not directly relevant to the issues that arise on this appeal. ***On 16th May 2000 the European Parliament and the Council of Ministers issued Directive 2000/26/EC, known as the 'Fourth Motor Insurance Directive'.*** *The Directive, which drew heavily on the Green Card system, lies at the heart of the present appeal.* ***Its primary purpose was to make it easier for victims of road traffic accidents to recover compensation by enabling them to pursue claims in their countries of residence against a representative of the insurer. At the same time the Directive required Member States to put in place legislation to give those injured in road accidents a right to make a claim directly against the driver's insurer. In order to provide further support for the system the Directive also required each Member State to establish a compensation body against which the victim could pursue a claim if the insurer's representative failed to respond promptly to the claim or the vehicle was not covered by insurance or could not be traced. I shall refer to this as the 'Fourth Directive'.***

Under the scheme established by the Fourth Directive the compensation body in the state where the injured person resides provides a person from whom he can recover if the driver's insurer fails to respond promptly to his claim or the driver is uninsured or a rel-

evant insurer cannot be identified. However, the compensation body is not the person ultimately responsible for bearing the loss, having a right to recover from the compensation body of the state in which the insurer is established (in the case of an insured vehicle) or against the guarantee fund of the state in which the vehicle is normally based (where the vehicle can be identified but there is no insurance) or of the state in which the accident took place (where the vehicle cannot be identified).

The following provisions of the Fourth Directive are of particular relevance to this appeal:

"Article 1

Scope

1. The objective of this Directive is to lay down special provisions applicable to injured parties entitled to compensation in respect of any loss or injury resulting from accidents occurring in a Member State other than the Member State of residence of the injured party which are caused by the use of vehicles insured and normally based in a Member State.

. . .

Article 4

Claims representatives

1. Each Member State shall take all measures necessary to ensure that all insurance undertakings . . . appoint a claims representative in each Member State other than that in which they have received their official authorisation. The claims representative shall be responsible for handling and settling claims arising from an accident in the cases referred to in Article 1. The claims representative shall be resident or established in the Member State where he is appointed.

. . .

Article 6

Compensation bodies

1. Each Member State shall establish or approve a compensation body responsible for providing compensation to injured parties in the cases referred to in Article 1.
Such injured parties may present a claim to the compensation body in their Member State of residence:
. . .

The compensation body shall take action within two months of the date when the injured party presents a claim for compensation to it . . .

. . . Member States may not allow the body to make the payment of compensation subject to any conditions other than those laid down in this Directive, in particular the injured party's establishing in any way that the person liable is unable or refuses to pay.

2. The compensation body which has compensated the injured party in his Member State of residence shall be entitled to claim reimbursement of the sum paid by way of compensation from the compensation body in the Member State of the insurance undertaking's establishment which issued the policy.

The latter body shall then be subrogated to the injured party in his rights against the person who caused the accident or his insurance undertaking in so far as the compensation body in the Member State of residence of the injured party has provided compensation for the loss or injury suffered. Each Member State is obliged to acknowledge this subrogation as provided for by any other Member State.

3. This Article shall take effect:

(a) after an agreement has been concluded between the compensation bodies established or approved by the Member States relating to their functions and obligations and the procedures for reimbursement;

. . .

Article 7

If it is impossible to identify the vehicle or if, within two months following the accident, it is impossible to identify the insurance undertaking, the injured party may apply for compensation from the compensation body in the Member State where he resides. *The compensation shall be provided in accordance with the provisions of Article 1 of [the Second Directive]. The compensation body shall then have a claim, on the conditions laid down in Article 6(2) of this Directive:*

(a) where the insurance undertaking cannot be identified: against the guarantee fund provided for in Article 1(4) of [the Second Directive] in the Member State where the vehicle is normally based;

(b) in the case of an unidentified vehicle: against the guarantee fund in the Member State in which the accident took place; . . . "

The Fourth Motor Insurance Directive Agreement

On 29th April 2002 the compensation bodies and guarantee funds in the Member States entered into an agreement know as the Fourth Motor Insurance Directive Agreement ("the Agreement") for the purposes of implementing the arrangements for which the Fourth Directive provided. The Agreement provided, among other things, as follows:

"3.4 Save as herein provided, the Compensation Body shall be the sole body responsible for compensating the injured party or his/her legal beneficiaries. It shall however,

— . . .

— *apply, when determining liability and assessing compensation, the applicable law of the country in which the accident occurred."*

A similar provision is to be found in clause 7.2.

The Regulations

The provisions of the Fourth Directive relating to compensation bodies were implemented by the Regulations. (The provisions for direct rights of action against insurers were implemented by the European Communities (Rights against Insurers) Regulations 2002.) Regulation 10 approves the MIB as the compensation body for the United Kingdom for the purposes of the Fourth Directive. *The important parts for present purposes are regulation 12(3) and (4) and regulation 13. Regulation 12 requires the compensation body to respond to a claim by a person resident in this country who has been injured in a road traffic accident abroad (for these purposes in another EEA State) involving a vehicle which is normally based abroad and insured through an establishment abroad. The material parts provide as follows:*

"12(3) ***If the injured party satisfies the compensation body as to the matters specified in paragraph (4), the compensation body shall indemnify the injured party in respect of the loss and damage described in paragraph (4)(b).***

(4) The matters referred to in paragraph (3) are—

(a) that a person whose liability for the use of the vehicle is insured by the insurer referred to in regulation 11(1)(c) is liable to the injured party in respect of the accident which is the subject of the claim, and

(b) the amount of loss and damage (including interest) that is properly recoverable in consequence of that accident by the

injured party from that person under the laws applying in that part of the United Kingdom in which the injured party resided at the date of the accident."

Regulation 13 gives a person resident in this country who has been injured in a road traffic accident abroad involving a vehicle which is normally based abroad a right to obtain compensation from the compensation body if it has proved impossible to identify the vehicle or an insurance undertaking which insures it. The material parts provide as follows:

"(1) This regulation applies where—

(a) an accident, caused by or arising out of the use of a vehicle which is normally based in an EEA State, occurs on the territory of —

(i) an EEA State other than the United Kingdom, or—

(ii) . . . and an injured party resides in the United Kingdom.

(b) . . . , and

(c) it has proved impossible—

(i) to identify the vehicle the use of which is alleged to have been responsible for the accident, or

(ii) . . . to identify an insurance undertaking which insures the use of the vehicle.

(2) Where this regulation applies—

(a) the injured party may make a claim for compensation from the compensation body, and

> *(b) the compensation body shall compensate the injured party in accordance with the provisions of Article 1 of the [Second Directive] as if it were the body authorised under paragraph 4 of that Article and the accident had occurred in Great Britain."*

The Claimant may usually submit a claim under the MIB's Green card scheme, and the link to the MIB website, which provides the information can be found here:- https://www.mib.org.uk/making-a-claim/accidents-in-the-uk-involving-a-foreign-registered-vehicle/before-making-a-claim/. **provided that proceedings have not already been commenced against the insurer.**

The MIB is the UK Green Card Bureau and so is the 'deemed' insurer of foreign registered vehicles in the UK. The MIB will be required to accept service of proceedings on behalf of the foreign motorist, provided the proceedings have not already been commenced against the insurer.

SI 2003/37 (which implements the Fourth directive into UK Law) sets out:-

> "***Compensation body for the United Kingdom 10.*** *MIB is approved as the compensation body for the United Kingdom for the purposes of the fourth motor insurance directive(a).*
>
> ***Entitlement to compensation where the insurer is identified***
>
> *11.—(1) This regulation and regulation 12 apply in a case where —*
>
> *(a) an injured party is resident in the United Kingdom,*
>
> *(b) that person claims to be entitled to compensation in respect of an accident occurring in an EEA State other than the United Kingdom or in a subscribing state, and*
>
> *(c) thelossorinjurytowhichtheclaimrelateshasbeencausedbyorarisesoutoftheuse of a vehicle which is—*

(i) normally based in an EEA State other than the United Kingdom, and

(ii) insured though an establishment in an EEA State other than the United Kingdom.

(2) Where this regulation applies, the injured party may make a claim for compensation from the compensation body if—

(a) he has not commenced legal proceedings against the insurer of the vehicle the use of which caused the accident, and

(b) either of the conditions set out in paragraph (3) is fulfilled.

(3) The conditions are—

(a) that the injured party has claimed compensation from the insurer of the vehicle or the insurer's claims representative and neither the insurer nor the claims representative has provided a reasoned reply to the claim within the period of three months after the date it was made;

(b) that the insurer has failed to appoint a claims representative in the United Kingdom, and the injured party has not claimed compensation directly from that insurer.

Response from the compensation body

12.—(1) Upon receipt of a claim for compensation under regulation 11, the compensation body shall immediately notify—

(a) the insurer of the vehicle the use of which is alleged to have caused the accident, or that insurer's claims representative;

(b) the foreign compensation body in the EEA State in which that insurer's establishment is situated; and

(c) if known, the person who is alleged to have caused the accident, that it has received a claim from the injured party and that it will respond to that claim within two months from the date on which the claim was received.

(2) The compensation body shall respond to a claim for compensation within two months of receiving the claim.

(3) If the injured party satisfies the compensation body as to the matters specified in paragraph (4), the compensation body shall indemnify the injured party in respect of the loss and damage described in paragraph (4)(b).

(4) The matters referred to in paragraph (3) are—

(a) that a person whose liability for the use of the vehicle is insured by the insurer referred to in regulation 11(1)(c) is liable to the injured party in respect of the accident which is the subject of the claim, and

(b) the amount of loss and damage (including interest) that is properly recoverable in consequence of that accident by the injured party from that person under the laws applying in that part of the United Kingdom in which the injured party resided at the date of the accident.

(a) See Article 6.

(5) The compensation body shall cease forthwith to act in respect of a claim as soon as it becomes aware that—

(a) the insurer referred to in regulation 11(1)(c), or the claims representative of that insurer, has made a reasoned response to the claim, or

(b) the injured party has commenced legal proceedings against the insurer.

Therefore, *Directive 2009/103/EC* of the European Parliament and of the Council of 16 September 2009 relates to insurance against civil liability in respect of the use of motor vehicles, and the enforcement of the obligation to insure against such liability. Article 18 says "***Direct right of action: Member States shall ensure that any party injured as a result of an accident caused by a vehicle covered by insurance as referred to in Article 3 enjoys a direct right of action against the insurance undertaking covering the person responsible against civil liability***" The Claimant *may rely upon Spedition Welter GmbH v Avanssur SA C-306/1,* where the CJEU considered a direct action claim under the direct right.

Further and/or in the alternative, the claimant could rely upon the *Fourth Motor Insurance Directive of 16 May 2000 (2000/26/EC), the domestic regulations enacted to comply with it, and the Fifth Motor Directive of 11 May 2005 (2005/14/EC).* Article 3 states "***Direct right of action***: *Each Member State shall ensure that injured parties referred to in Article 1 in accidents within the meaning of that provision enjoy a direct right of action against the insurance undertaking covering the responsible person against civil liability".* The Claimant could also rely upon Brussels I COUNCIL REGULATION (EC) No 44/2001 of 22 December 2000 and Article 9.1 which states:-

> *"An insurer domiciled in a Member State may be sued:*
>
> *(a) in the courts of the Member State where he is domiciled, or (b) in another Member State, in the case of actions brought by the policyholder, the insured or a beneficiary, in the courts for the place where the plaintiff is domiciled.* Article 11(2) states: "*Articles 8, 9 and 10 shall apply to actions brought by the injured party directly against the insurer, where such direct actions are permitted".* The preamble to the Fifth Directive states at paragraph 24:- *Under Article 11(2) read in conjunction with Article 9(1)(b) of Council Regulation (EC) No 44/2001 of 22 December 2000 on jurisdiction and the recognition and enforcement of judgments in civil and com-*

> *mercial matters (1), injured parties may bring legal proceedings against the civil liability insurance provider in the Member State in which they are domiciled".*

Rome II Regulation (EC) No 864/2007 of the European Parliament and of the Council of 11 July 2007, is intended to impose a uniform approach within Europe for determining applicable law. *The Rome Convention (brought into English law by the Contracts (Applicable Law) Act 1990)* provides that the law applicable to a contract shall govern "*within the limits of the powers conferred on the court by its procedural law, the consequences of breach, including the assessment of damages in so far as it is governed by rules of 20 law*" (article 10(1)(c)) It applies even where a defendant is domiciled the EC. The CJEU ruled in *Homawoo v GMF Assurances SA C-412/10* that its provisions apply to an accident occurring after 11 January 2009. *Article 4 of Rome II (EC 864 No 2007)* sets the applicable law "*shall be the law of the country in which the damage occurs*". That same law will govern substantive issues of liability, causation, contributory negligence, legal presumptions and burdens of proof, and, by Art 15(c) "*the existence, the nature and the assessment of damage or the remedy claimed*".

The combination of the European Legislation above, enacted into the law of England and Wales confers a direct right of action upon a foreign insurer who is a signatory to Rome II.

It should be noted that Schedule 4 of the *Civil Jurisdiction and Judgments Act 1982* applies as between those domiciled to decide whether a claim is brought in England, Scotland or Northern Ireland.

Rome II and RTA Accidents Abroad

Sections 11 and 12 of the *Private International Law (Miscellaneous Provisions) Act 1995*. The general rule, pursuant to section 11, is that the law to be applied by the English Court is, "*the law of the country in which the events constituting the tort or delict in question occur*".

Rome II is the law which applies to all RTAs, which occur in a country that is a signatory. European Regulation 864/2007 or "*Rome II*" is one of the most important developments for international personal injury claims in recent years. It creates a standard set of rules for European Courts to use when dealing with non-contractual cases involving a cross-border element, for example if a driver was injured in a Road Traffic Accident whilst travelling abroad. It intended to harmonise the rules determining which law should apply when more than one jurisdiction is involved.

The general rule of Rome II essentially states that the applicable law to be used is the law of the country in which the damage occurred. This is the default position which applies to all countries in the European Union, with the exception of Denmark.

This general rule will not apply if the liable party and the injured party are residents of the same country (in which case the laws of that country will apply, even if the accident happened abroad).

The general rule will also not apply if it is determined that the case is clearly more closely connected to another country; in which case the law of that country will apply. Rome II also, subject to some restrictions, allows the parties to choose to apply the laws of a different country provided an agreement to this effect is entered into.

The relevant sections of Rome II are set out as follows:-

> *Article 4*
>
> *General rule*
>
> *1. Unless otherwise provided for in this Regulation,* ***the law applicable to a non-contractual obligation arising out of a tort/delict shall be the law of the country in which the damage occurs irrespective of the country in which the event giving rise to the damage occurred and irrespective of the country or coun- tries in which the indirect consequences of that event occur.***

2. However, where the person claimed to be liable and the person sustaining damage both have their habitual residence in the same country at the time when the damage occurs, the law of that country shall apply.

3. Where it is clear from all the circumstances of the case that the tort/delict is manifestly more closely connected with a country other than that indicated in paragraphs 1 or 2, the law of that other country shall apply. *A manifestly closer connection with another country might be based in particular on a pre- existing relationship between the parties, such as a contract, that is closely connected with the tort/delict in question.*

<u>What about the assessment of damages/quantum?</u>

Regulation (15) (2) says:-

Article 15

Scope of the law applicable

The law applicable to non-contractual obligations under this Regulation shall govern in particular:

(a) the basis and extent of liability, including the determination of persons who may be held liable for acts performed by them;

(b) the grounds for exemption from liability, any limitation of liability and any division of liability;

(c) the existence, the nature and the assessment of damage or the remedy claimed;

(d) within the limits of powers conferred on the court by its procedural law, the measures which a court may take to pre- vent or

terminate injury or damage or to ensure the provision of compensation;

(e) the question whether a right to claim damages or a remedy may be transferred, including by inheritance;

(f) persons entitled to compensation for damage sustained personally;

(g) liability for the acts of another person;

(h) the manner in which an obligation may be extinguished and rules of prescription and limitation, including rules relating to the commencement, interruption and suspension of a period of prescription or limitation.

The High Court in *Jacobs* held that the approach to the interpretation and application of Rome II should be broad and purposive, and that the purpose of Rome II was achieved in the case of a tort by the application of the general rule in Article 4(1), **which meant the applicable law would be that of the country where the damage occurred.** Therefore in such cases, the Claimant will probably require expert evidence of an appropriate lawyer to confirm the law of the local jurisdiction. The position was helpfully set out in the case of **ROBERT CHARLES SYRED v (1) POWSZECNNY ZAKLAD UBEZPIECZEN (PZU) SA (2) WACLAW BEDNORZ (3) HDI-GERLING INDUSTRIE VERSICHERUNG AG (2016)**, which found that Polish Law was the correct approach to contributory negligence and quantum:-

"*Contributory negligence : the law*

The issue of contributory negligence arises from the admitted fact that Mr Syred was not wearing a seat belt. The first question concerns Polish law in this respect.

On this issue, I heard the expert evidence of Mr Janusz Tomczak (instructed on behalf of Mr Syred) and Dr Maciej Rewienski (instructed on behalf of the Defendants). ***Mr Tomczak is an***

advocate at the Polish Bar with 8 years experience as a litigator in the firm of Wardinski & Partners. Dr Rewienski qualified as an advocate in 2004, has a Ph.D in law and has been a partner in his firm (KKR) since 2008. He has substantial experience in conducting road traffic claims in the Polish civil courts and told me that he had conducted some 6000 such cases since 2008.

There is no dispute between these experts that a rear seat passenger who fails to wear a seat belt is at fault and negligent for the purpose of the passenger's civil claims for compensation under Polish law.

The experts also agree that the next question in Polish law is whether such negligence caused the injuries or made them worse. However, they disagree as to the burden of proof in this respect.

Contributory negligence : the deduction

If all the injuries and their consequences would have been avoided, my deduction from the total award, applying the Judge's law of Article 362 and taken account of the experts' guidance on Polish law and practice, would have been 25%. *However it is clear that the overwhelming predominant injury is to the brain; and the Defendants have not established that that injury would have been avoided or lessened if a seat belt had been worn. Furthermore the largest items of loss, i.e. past and future loss of earnings, past and future case management and future care are entirely attributable to that injury and it plays the entire or a substantial part in many other heads of award. The aortic tear was a very serious injury but on my findings causes no distinct pecuniary loss.*

I have considered whether to try and make an individual calculation against each head of loss but have concluded that the right approach, consistent with Polish law and practice, is to have an overall percentage which reflects the predominance of the brain injury. *Taking all these considerations into account I conclude that* *the overall deduction for contributory negligence from the total award should be 5%"*

"By virtue of the provisions of 'Rome II'1 the issues of contributory negligence (Art.15(a) and (b)) and quantum ('the existence, the nature and the assessment of damage...' : Art. 15(c)) fall to be determined by Polish law. However the burden of pleading and proving that foreign law differs from English law falls on the party seeking to rely on the foreign law, in this case the Defendants. Determination of foreign law is a question of fact for the Court. Matters of evidence and procedure are governed by English law (Art.1(3))"

In TIFFANY MORENO v MOTOR INSURERS' BUREAU (2015) The court was required to determine a preliminary issue in relation to the applicable law for the assessment of compensation payable by the defendant MIB to the claimant following a road traffic accident in Greece. The Court said:-

79.*"The Defendant says, with some force, that given the fundamental change in the landscape, what is required is the interpretation of the 2003 Regulations so that Rome II is given effect. If that argument were accepted, the words in Regulation 13 would not provide a provision in effective conflict with Rome II. The Defendant also has force in its argument that in Jacobs the Court of Appeal has accepted that Rome II Art 4 dictates the choice of law on the issue of liability, but then has not applied it to the issue of compensation.*

80. ***As I indicated at the outset of this judgment, I am bound by the two Court of Appeal authorities of Jacobs and Bloy. I would not consider that there is force in the Defendant's case that the Regulations were misinterpreted as they stood. However I am of the view that the effect of Rome II on the correct interpretation required to bring Regulation 13 into conformity with Article 4 gives the Defendant's arguments that Jacobs was wrongly decided, and that the approach of Owen J at first instance in Jacobs***

> *should be endorsed, very considerable force. Whether they are of sufficient force to achieve a different result will be for others to determine.*
>
> *83. Given that the only issue remaining between the parties is the assessment of the compensation payable, I am therefore bound to answer the issue question thus: it is to be assessed in accordance with the law of England and Wales".*

The High Court in other words was bound by *Jacobs* to conclude that compensation was to be assessed under English law in claims brought in England in Wales under the Motor Vehicles (Compulsory Insurance) (Information Centre and Compensation Body) Regulations 2003 reg.13 against the MIB by persons from England and Wales who had been injured in other EU states by culpable but uninsured or unidentified drivers.

In ROBERT BACON v NACIONAL SUIZA CIA SEGUROS Y RESEGUROS SA (2010), the Court the Court held that Spanish law would govern the nature and the assessment of damage, or the remedy claimed, because of the applicability of Regulation 864/2007.

Limitation

The *Foreign Limitation Periods Act 1984* sets out:-

> ***Application of foreign limitation law.***
>
> *(1) Subject to the following provisions of this Act, where in any action or proceedings in a court in England and Wales the law of any other country falls (in accordance with rules of private international law applicable by any such court) to be taken into account in the determination of any matter—*
>
> *(a) the law of that other country relating to limitation shall apply in respect of that matter for the purposes of the action or proceedings [F1, subject to [F2sections 1A and 1B]]; and*

(b) except where that matter falls within subsection (2) below, the law of England and Wales relating to limitation shall not so apply.

(2) A matter falls within this subsection if it is a matter in the determination of which both the law of England and Wales and the law of some other country fall to be taken into account.

(3) The law of England and Wales shall determine for the purposes of any law applicable by virtue of subsection (1)(a) above whether, and the time at which, proceedings have been commenced in respect of any matter; and accordingly, section 35 of the M1Limitation Act 1980 (new claims in pending proceedings) shall apply in relation to time limits applicable by virtue of subsection (1)(a) above as it applies in relation to time limits under that Act.

(4) A court in England and Wales, in exercising in pursuance of subsection (1)(a) above any discretion conferred by the law of any other country, shall so far as practicable exercise that discretion in the manner in which it is exercised in comparable cases by the courts of that other country.

(5) In this section "law", in relation to any country, shall not include rules of private international law applicable by the courts of that country or, in the case of England and Wales, this Act.

However, this will not apply in Rome II case as section 8 says:-

[F78

Disapplication of sections 1, 2 and 4 where [F8the law applicable to limitation is determined by other instruments]

(1) Where in proceedings in England and Wales the law of a country other than England and Wales falls to be taken into account by virtue of any choice of law rule contained in [F9the Rome I Regulation or] the Rome II Regulation, sections 1, 2 and 4 above shall not apply in respect of that matter.

> ***In subsection (1) the " Rome I Regulation " means Regulation (EC) No. 593/2008 of the European Parliament and of the Council on the law applicable to contractual obligations, including that Regulation as applied by regulation 5 of the Law Applicable to Contractual Obligations** (England and Wales and Northern Ireland) Regulations 2009 (conflicts solely between the laws of different parts of the United Kingdom or between one or more parts of the United Kingdom and Gibraltar).*
>
> *(2) In subsection (1) the " Rome II Regulation " means Regulation (EC) No. 864/2007 of the European Parliament and of the Council on the law applicable to non-contractual obligations, including that Regulation as applied by regulation 6 of the Law Applicable to Non-Contractual Obligations (England and Wales and Northern Ireland) Regulations 2008 (conflicts solely between the laws of different parts of the United Kingdom or between one or more parts of the United Kingdom and Gibraltar).*

In order words limitation would be the law of England and Wales, as the 1984 Act will not apply.

CONCLUSIONS AND THE SMALL CLAIMS TRACK

It is a strong possibility that the small claims track will rise to £5,000 or at least be raised by a considerable amount in either October 2017 or April 2018. It is arguable, however, that even if the small claims track rises to £5,000, accidents abroad cases (including Athens, Montreal or the 1992 Regulations), will be too complex for the small claims track given:-

a) The 1992 Regulations require evidence of local standards and the small claims track does not make provision for this.

b) The cases (Athens/Montreal/1992 local standards) are complex.

c) The cases involve accidents outside the jurisdiction.

d) The quantum issues can be complex and involved.

e) The claims require the skill and knowledge of a specialist lawyer.

However, this may not apply to holiday sickness cases. The outcome in relation to such claims remains to be seen and is highly speculative at the time of writing.

Accidents abroad and travel claims will hopefully provide another area of work for PI Lawyers post reforms. However, one does need to be aware these are potentially complex cases and there are many traps that the unwary Lawyer can fall into such as differing limitation periods.

One also has to bare in mind that post Jackson and QOCS / Fundamental dishonesty is now a significant concern. Firms undertaking travel claims (and in particular holiday sickness) need to have detailed fraud checks before accepting cases on CFA such as:

a) Facebook / social media checks to see if what the client is telling you is correct.

b) Cross checks with medical records to check medical causation and consistency.

c) Identity and address checks to check the client is who they say they are! Experian soft footprint credit checks are very useful.

d) Other cross checking against documents such as employment records / accident report forms.

If the Claimant's credibility is in doubt, these claims may not be suitable for a CFA.

MORE BOOKS BY LAW BRIEF PUBLISHING

'A Practical Guide to Personal Injuries in Sport' by Adam Walker & Patricia Leonard
'Baby Steps: A Guide to Maternity Leave and Maternity Pay' by Leah Waller
'The Queen's Counsel Lawyer's Omnibus: 20 Years of Cartoons from the Times 1993-2013' by Alex Steuart Williams

These books and more are available to order online direct from the publisher at www.lawbriefpublishing.com, where you can also read free sample chapters. For any queries, contact us on 0844 587 2383 or mail@lawbriefpublishing.com.

Our books are also usually in stock at www.amazon.co.uk with free next day delivery for Prime members, and at good legal bookshops such as Hammicks and Wildy & Sons.

We are regularly launching new books in our series of practical day-to-day practitioners' guides. Visit our website and join our free newsletter to be kept informed.

www.ingramcontent.com/pod-product-compliance
Lightning Source LLC
LaVergne TN
LVHW022051200926
848481LV00003B/870
9781911035022